I0693358

THE GAIA HYPOTHESIS

CULTIVATED MAN/ NATURAL PLANET

Elissa Rubenstein

BALBOA.PRESS

A DIVISION OF HAY HOUSE

Balboa Press books may be ordered through booksellers or by contacting:

Balboa Press
A Division of Hay House
1663 Liberty Drive
Bloomington, IN 47403
www.balboapress.com
844-682-1282

Print information available on the last page.

ISBN: 978-1-9822-2806-4 (sc)
ISBN: 978-1-9822-2807-1 (e)

Library of Congress Control Number: 2019906858

Balboa Press rev. date: 06/16/2023

CHAPTER ONE

IMBALANCED EARTH

Imbalance is a problem on Earth. This is demonstrated by the Gaia philosophy that states that one's work should be rewarded by a similarity in response. A work day should lead to an answered prayer at the end of the day, and all life is sustained as the work earning daily bread is put forth to aid oneself and others in exchange each day for sustenance. Then there is harmony between work and effort and then reward.

The Earthly imbalance is seen among the family of man. Animals we know work daily sowing and reaping, dwelling, multiplying and nurturing, performing the daily work of budgeting resources, habitat-building and sowing the seeds of vegetation, and then resting and hibernating in peace with their families and societies. People on the other hand often receive much more for sustenance than they would ever need and more than they could ever work for. So many systems exist on Earth in harmony, balanced in a never-ending flow, mathematically perfect, intertwined with other life systems of the planet, together providing nourishment of all need and want – and often untold joy – that work in perfection mirroring outwardly to us the beauty of the planet.

But so much else falls out of regularity and even logic, garishly, the systems of man, not organically grown and a part of the perfect mechanism, but separate and inconsistent, uneconomical, wasteful and not mechanically logical. For example, those who have so much to eat in unhealthy and gluttonous amounts embarrass our worth when those without sustenance have none, which runs antithetical to the Earth motto. Those prayerful souls close to the church and to God who bring so much softening spirit to the planet environs oppose a separate demand of some men and women who choose lives of crime and dissipation. Another system of man has wrought slavery, forcing some to work hard and long for no reward while others reap the rewards of others' work in amazing quantities. Then there is the stock market, selling a non-ending glut of goods in quantities impossible to consume and at a rate of speed faster than any mouth can eat. At the same time a poverty of even basic necessity exists. Just the same, some nations are supported in their every aspiration, with their citizens able to have anything they desire, while at the same time other nations have so little and bear fruit infrequently. Indeed, one sees man's mini-systems opposing the system that guides the planet in its day-to-day ability to procreate fruit and purpose throughout history.

To survive, the planet cared for itself, all of its forms, colors and aspects. Each pattern of thought, being and motion, each chemical reaction, each turn of the globe, was synchronized to work harmoniously intertwined with a whole system of other forms within the same boundaries and even outside worlds and planets to form a consistent unique and individualistic life consistent and dependable for sustaining also a universal life everywhere today and tomorrow and able to evolve to form a unique and consistent evolution. To move in a way antithetical to the dream

of maturing in a way that consistently manifests God's

plan, whatever that may hold as we change every day,

is stupid and foolish, and that is the path only of those

seeking untold wealth in advance of the whole bearing

fruit together. Those who seem oppositional to Earth's

organic time frame, and who reap more prematurely

before the reward to all is known each day, hurt the

will of all beings on Earth and then cause everyone

else to adjust everywhere to this imbalance and loss

of their own reward and then cause further disease

and disorder. When all is said and done, the planet

must fight harder to heal because some are fighting

others who are stolen from to sustain their wealth. It

is inconceivable that we should die or go hungry but

it seems that we might.

CHAPTER TWO

THE GAIA HYPOTHESIS, THE EARTH AND MAN'S MARKETPLACE

Are man's economic values antithetical to Earthly law as set forth in the believed governance of our planet known as the Gaia Hypothesis? The Gaia hypothesis proposes that our planet functions as a single organism that maintains conditions necessary for survival of all life. Through exchange, reaping and sowing, give and take, the planet lives in homeostasis and harmony of all life which is intertwined on Earth in order for all life here to be fruitful and multiply, protecting and serving all life. Indeed, all Earthly organisms – all life on our planet together intertwined as one form – called the biosphere – interact with their surroundings to form a self-regulating, complex, constantly harmonizing system that contributes to maintaining the conditions necessary to sustained procreation of the planet. Also, the total ensemble (including humans) of living organisms constituting the biosphere (all living beings on Earth seen together as one union) act as a single entity together through thought and action and regulate the Earth's chemical composition, surface PH, vegetation and other life, food choices and even climate.

What these actions demonstrate is that all beings alive on our planet – animal, plant, insect, reptile and human – live in harmony working to feed and sustain and nurture one another, living in stasis and harmony where all beings are safe together, bringing the best results for all and sustaining the every need of all by allotting all Earthly resources for all life on the planet in shares exactly mirroring what each life form needs at any given time to live. That harmony, this author believes, means all life together work toward sustaining other lives who share as neighbors the whole Earth environment. When one part of the harmonious reservoir of life is out of synch with the rest, that disintegration hurts those life forms that might depend upon that one part, or on the goods and resources that were not there for them that day as expected, and the whole then must suffer because then a chain is broken where those who experience a sudden lack cannot function well supporting those others that receive sustenance in some way from that broken down area. As an integrated chain, humans, animals, plants, insects and reptiles alike sustain other life in their taking part of the joined Earthly work keeping a planet functioning; if one part is out of synchronicity, then other forms' needs will not be met and the working whole will break down.

When one considers insatiable waste of food and other resources our planet has to offer all life now and in the future that occurs when rampant consumerism controls man's marketplaces, we see much waste of planetary gifts meant to sustain all life as they are needed by life in a certain time frame. If for example, a company or life form were to take more than their share before the taken goods are needed, that causes imbalance to all life.

This shows that the Gaia Hypothesis promoting understanding of harmonious interrelated systems and the marketplace of man must mirror the Earth's natural marketplace of sowing and reaping in exact correlation to the work given and reward taken by all life organic to the planet's true law. Earth is a planet of many interrelated systems, from the simple to the complex, and one sees a similar thought pattern threading through nature or environmental systems and social systems. This deeper understanding of Earthly life through interconnection between all life that must care for all life in order to survive and for the Earth to survive is defined as systems thinking, and this is considered the process of understanding how systems guiding all life activities on our planet influence one another within the whole, with all following the same pattern as created under the Gaia Hypothesis.

In nature, systems thinking describes the Earth's daily operations of sustaining life as a holistic system where all parts are interconnected and where individual forms of life cannot act as entities that oppose the sustenance of life of other beings connected to them. Under this theory, how the individual parts function within the whole is less important than the evolution of our home – the Earth as a whole – taking into account the needs of all life and sustaining all life now and in the future as we endure and as we evolve.

Our market economy, because it represents a mirror of and a system acting within the whole, of man's chosen form of work and reward, must imitate the Earth system as described under Gaia's Hypothesis, imitating biological give and take between all life together – sustaining all as one family, making the societies on Earth mirror the guiding philosophy that makes our planet work for millennia to safely harbor multitudinous life. Indeed, the one spirit of Earth enveloping and regulating not just the natural life of the Earth's interior and then animal and plant life on the surface, also must guide and regulate human endeavor. Just as the Earth's many natural lives make up one organism operating to nurture the overall spirit of all natural life on the planet, the same spirit – as one thought – must also guide the life of man as he works with others to arrange exchange of goods and services. Therefore, marketplaces built to sustain lives of men, plants, animals and other life should mirror the philosophy that adheres to the ideal that all must participate only in activities that promote the betterment of all populations.

When man's marketplaces act differently and not in synchronicity with the planet's harmonious inclusion of all life together participating equally and earning reward equally, allowing some to take more than others and more than they need, which infringes on another's share at any given moment, the Earth must produce more for those whose share has been stolen. Then there is planetary waste and disharmony and disease. Then the planet suffers into an unhealthy state where perfect harmonious regulation of all Earth social and environmental systems are disrupted. Further, when some take unrelentingly and hugely more than they need and waste goods and services from the Earth that are meant to sustain life of all beings, those acting this way control more resources that are truly the resources of others sometimes and with their riches and influence then control ideologies of those needing those forms of sustenance and those holding the power often do this in a way to satisfy selfishness, waste, opportunism and thievery, and then those come to control many who then suffer on Earth, where under the Gaia Hypothesis, none should suffer. This author believes that this behavior leads to a dangerous cataclysm and disruption of Earth's lawful functioning as a system where all life works equally as their circumstance allows and reap equally as to exactly what they need. When man is taking more than is needed at any given time and is not living in harmony with – and indeed is interrupting the harmony of – natural Earth law protecting and sustaining all life equally, sustainability problems result within the natural and social Earth systems and then breakdowns in Earthly flow of happiness, health and wealth occur for all. And the spirit of our planet does know who is out of alignment within the whole and wreaking havoc on all life who may suffer at the hands of few.

When considering man's hand in either sustaining the Gaia Hypothesis or rejecting it, we pray all will reconsider stock market mentalities (which by the very definition of the words mean to stock pile goods in advance in an area not truly their home and natural and most healthy location and to horde them, in order to sell them in a separate system away from the truthful Earth governance). Such mentalities expect exorbitant and cruel and unusual levels of fruits to be horded by some while others suffer and are subjugated today and many continue to suffer – with growing and added suffering as such a system comes to take root – tomorrow. The conclusion to be drawn is that the marketplace of man on Earth's topography should exactly mirror the evolution of Earth's natural laws, imitating the functioning of a natural world that seeks to include all life equally in participation with our home and in receipt of gifts of health, well-being, friendship and harmonious interconnection of all life. If ever one is sick, then – due to our immense interconnectivity with all life – we all are sick and then all life becomes disharmonious and then cannot provide for each other as we would normally work together to exchange between us all that we need. Finally, when the Earthly systems of protection, nurturing and holistic sustenance is disrupted, which leads to suffering of all life from breakdowns within the natural and social operating systems, the Earthly spirit – which encompasses our heavens – suffers. And that causes complete collapse of happiness of all beings because the heavenly realm which we count on to provide spiritual sustenance when we suffer then is also broken and cannot nurture a planet and people and animal population in trauma.

CHAPTER THREE

DELAY

When the Earth was new and functioning as God intended, and all of its natural systems and cycles performed in perfect health, a harmonious whole existed with sustenance of all life within its globe the norm. As it hummed through every day, there was procreation of life and sustenance of life in equal measure. Cycles of freshwater, salinity, phosphorus, nitrogen and carbon flowed in cyclical motion throughout time-held paths over the course of a set and time-held number of years each. The nourishment needed to sustain the parts of the planet in motion – its animate life forms of man, fish, insect, bird, mammal – and the nourishment needed to sustain the parts of the planet in stasis – rock, soil, vegetation – was plentiful. And as the life of the planet evolved through each day, doing its work and receiving its reward, all encompassed within the youthful and eternal spirit of Earth – the heavens above and the soil and water and solid rock below, made untold joy prevalent. The evolutionary periods of growth of the planet developed; certain features of Earth shone and developed; all helped create the whole that exists and that was in existence at any given time – a home of so many assets and features to enjoy.

These periods of Earthly evolution include: from a heated rock thrown out from the Sun, over time our planet evolved through periods of cooling. Throughout those periods, metals developed, then rock developed, then proteins and sugars and carbohydrates (or food) became evident. As the planet continued to cool, then land developed. From such growth, ecosystems were made possible because such interesting and varied conditions contained within the whole allowed for the concocting of a store of possibilities from which to paint a picture of individual choice and life and as a whole to together paint a plan. The planet continued to cool and sulfurs and vapors and other chemicals brought stability, sustenance, happiness and elevated thought appeared. Finally from this wealth of protective environments and sustenance and growing consciousness separate from our origin – the Sun – life itself began with the formation of hard shell bodies, bones and phosphorous, membrane. These in turn brought life forward with development of mammals such as fish and animals and man who could think again separately from the planet under their feet but also could connect the developing interior planetary thought to the father above through thought on the topography that could intermingle prayer of the father into their own lives and bring such to the interior of the planet that could then know the intentions of our creator to help us evolve. It is this then that became man and animal life purpose.

Through the developmental periods of Earth, animate (or mobile) life evolved as the planet's stationary parts stabilized; these expressions of life were complemented by the things around them close by in the locations in which they were born. Developing from early stage to growth to maturity, mobile life partook of the immediate environment to survive and then through cycles of exchange relationship with others nearby – as life began an "exchange" cycle – life began to bring in sustenance to itself and then release back something after. And through this process life among a group evolved. The parts of the developing planet that were taken into the life of the mobilizing life forms allowed these mobile forms of life to evolve, while other parts of the earth perhaps mobilized to join correlating other parts to begin cycles of different forms of elemental chains that needed to come together and form pathways. One can only assume that all of this activity was governed by the Creator. Through these patterns of organization of the planet – first to create the cycling patterns of our elements such as water and carbon and nitrogen etc. – the planet began its first series of exchanges since each cycling elemental flow in some way corresponded to and was made to harmonize perfectly with other cycles developing. Such perfect harmony of the elemental pathways of a developing planet show perfect levels of exchange between flowing life and more stationary life to sustain the whole being.

Today's Earth could be as creative and sustaining of all animate and inanimate life and supportive of all of its cycles in perfection. Indeed, today we could be witnessing equal number of miraculous events as was recorded in years previous. We could be surrounded by untold mysteries of creation and untold riches of possibility – now only limited by our stagnation in our planet and in our lifestyles. This is because when our planetary cycles are harmonized in synch with each other perfectly and through patterns accepted and within specified time frames together, beginning and completing at correct timeframes, that is when the planet is truly functioning perfectly – with all of its elements humming through their 1000 year cycles in harmony with the other pathways of elemental flow complementing such. When such ease of planetary functioning occurs, a cleaner planet comes into being because the precise timing of elemental cycling – such as the exact 1000-year water cycle of all waters on the planet – which assures that the water is moving within a pathway and timeframe held in place since our beginnings and within which pattern cleansing of water is occurring continuously. If such were occurring today, not just in the cycling pattern of our water but in all elements and all life, there would be many many more options to choose from in terms of the types of lifestyles available to lead, not to mention untold riches in terms of longevity of life, happiness, health and well-being and finally, the experiencing of the true ultimate potential life on Earth, offering every form of being a perfect healthy life. However, man has chosen to limp along and even die many many years too young and through a pattern of dull sameness and uneventful monotony not changing and not evolving because we are now mirroring exactly the lack of elemental flow and harmony within the elemental flow of water, carbon, nitrogen, etc. due to our over-abundant lifestyle and extraction of so much from the animal life available here and the extraction of so much from the inner core of the planet to build up so much on top of the ground in overwhelmingly large cities and towns. Because of our overwhelming stock-piling of goods once safely and harmoniously stored inside the Earth, now shown in our topography, we have used many of our resources in a way that has depleted many cyclical patterns. It is the time right now that this expression of man's out of synch methods not correlative to the truth of Earth's cycling patterns must change. We must find ways to stop the extravagant taking of the inner core of the planet out to the top of the planet and we must stop the killing of animal life, also taking away a cycle of life on the planet more valuable to the overall safe-keeping of all planetary cycling than man may realize. Because of these two factors of overabundant extraction of inanimate life and animate life, away from their true life as governed by the Creator, we have chopped up our planetary evolutionary cycling patterns and this has led to stagnation and pollution and disease and disarray and finally to a calamity of suffering and war and strife here. People should live as long as a full elemental cycle – 1000 years – but somehow, because we are a cycle within the whole being, a joined part of all cycles, all out or synchronous functioning, we too are polluted and toxic and even violent. Additionally, with such out of harmony patterns existing, we live in a constant pattern of delay. While the cycles of water and carbon move in not healthful ways, we must wait longer for these flowing elements, and all flows, to bring any form of harmony – if harmony can be found at all – to our lives. On the other hand, on a perfectly attuned functioning planet, cycles of life in perfection bring an immediacy of happiness and joy and fulfillment with them to the individual life, which pattern must correlate to the overall patterns. Therefore, one must conclude that we live in a state of utter illness and shortened lifespan and overall ill health and stalemate instead of receiving into our daily existence a steady flow of corresponding gifts to the thoughts we generate out to our environment and out to others in our work.

Delay is our prevalence. We pray and expect prayers to be answered at a later date. We offer our spirit to God in hopes our death even far afield will not be terrifying. We save our money and do not enjoy it now with a continuous daily gift for fear that our retirement will not allow for enough to sustain us or because we must save well in advance for college tuition. We eat foods and drink beverages now in hope that our health and appearance will change tomorrow. So much of modern life is creating something today in the hope that something resulting in some form of far-off dream in our mind will appear later. This imbalance of a life of unhappiness working overly hard today matching the need to fill up the losses that are within our planetary whole now, only to receive a little something of nothing in our retirement, is a far-off reality completely destitute of what our planet truly can provide. We therefore live in a state of constant delay and even delay preparation of a spiritual knowledge of life until the last minute when we feel it is time to consider that death may be looming.

If our planet's processes of creativity are sluggish, that may be directly related to an under-abundance of natural resources available to purvey the necessary result of each labor. An insatiable appetite for the delights of the Earth without recourse or consideration of just how much a planet can offer each day to those of such inclination has had a negative impact among men, and the acceptance of the over-consuming financial institution the stock market with undue and unreal levels of exchange of money with no actual commodity exchanging concurrently shows the selfishness and greed of many men which must later and concurrently and continuously lead to a correlation of constant taking from the Earth's abundance and store, taking such from the direct multitudinous functioning layers and cycles and processes of the planet and in essence cutting through these with so much machinery. Since the days of the start of the stock market the days also of imperialistic tendencies arose, whereby men developed tendencies to travel elsewhere, away from home, and then thieve from others, to subjugate them by owning their sustenance, to need to have more than those others in order to force them to do what those in power expected them to do. This risen tendency to travel into others' homes and thieve and then subject those who may have lived in those places for many eons began a system antithetical to the Gaia Hypothesis in which all parts are equally joined. Those forcing their will on innocent others and thieving in order to own their sustenance expected undue levels of work and pillage of innocent life in exchange for nothing in return. From this original deviation, so much has gone wrong with the inner and topographical functioning of our planet, causing mini-system after mini-system to develop in spiraling pattern out of control, spiraling away from the innate necessary workings of the planet for it to survive. In this author's opinion, by the year 2000, and the war that came from the bombing of New York, deep thinking began in the West which began in many ways to take stock of planetary problems. Those included the inhumane daily minute-by-minute slaughter of innocent animal life, desertification, drought, soil loss, heat, pollution, consumerism run amuck and a system that started many years ago that had finally put in place instead of a planet made for wilderness areas and sacred spaces for wildlife – the pollinators and habitat-builders of the planet, its caretakers – a planet meant only to satisfy the desires of man for control -- for farmlands instead of wetlands and forests and for animal husbandry whereby their innate abilities were trained away from multiplying growing cultivating and building a planet in God's plan wild in favor of a cultivated man-controlled Earth, leading us to catastrophe.

Therefore, while in the beginnings the power of the Creator and then our planet may have shaped our environs and our souls and caused us to develop in ways certain to act that reflected back the intention and correct functioning of the whole, over time, however, a group of men took the reins away from God in planetary functioning and its ability to sustain life collapsed. From that small group many things arose that was a mirror of their subjugation: war, hording, weaponry, crime, hostility, separatism, prejudice, slavery. Therefore, since man is now in control, it is up to man now to relinquish where his tendencies have become misshapen and to allow the higher thought to again regain its stature. The weather extremism we have experienced throughout this reign of separation from the true Earth plan – evidenced by earthquake, avalanche, hurricane, monsoon, tornado, for example, where life is killed indeed by the planet in fury, is pure evidence of Earths' hostility toward its topography and actions taking place there and its growing emotional need to take control over us here at the ground floor. There is no alternative to man but to abide by the swirling education around us being shown daily in the weather patterns. Those patterns show the emotional well-being or lack thereof of the planet's interior, and where there is weather extremism and cataclysm there is also too much havoc being wreaked on the Earth interior for want of riches and continued control over innocent life.

The best first way to start to reclaim our innate true nature is to stop the slaughter of animals. That daily painful blood-letting is the most hideous of events showing how people can watch on a daily basis the slaughter of innocent life without recourse or care. If this one activity were to cease, then peaceful reclamation can occur.

CHAPTER FOUR

IS OUR ECONOMY ECONOMICAL?

When one thinks of the word "economy," two ideas
come to mind. One, the idea of thrift and an activity
of finding the best possible value for the cost allotted,
and two, the functioning of a marketplace based upon
the supply and demand of goods and services to fill a
need or demand for those products. Therefore, when
one considers our economy, one must remember the
definition of the term: a creative environment where
the necessary goods and services are allocated to a
consuming population, offering the most efficient and

effective fulfillment of the need for those products and services, at the lowest possible cost or at a cost truly matching the intrinsic value of the good or service provided. A truly economical economic system is one, therefore, that functions in a healthy manner and then finds demand of products and services and the level of products and services manufactured at each given moment to be equal. The efficiency and effectiveness of a truly economical economic system therefore is needed in absolute terms for a marketplace to function in a way in which it will not at times break down. If more products and services exist than a buying public needs and demands or less products and services exist than a buying public needs and demands, then a marketplace is either one, full of waste of our precious Earth resources which stay truly fresh and hygienic and most healthful if left in place until they are needed or two, not matching the need for sustaining all life and leaving some to suffer without nourishment hydration or shelter. Additionally, if more products sit on the shelves than the demand or need for such warrants, then the cost of those products would need to be lower than their true worth for those to sell, and when one considers a products' worth (or price) being lowered on the store shelf, then one must also correlate that the public might buy something that they do not need that truly has a higher worth in its origin location and will now move from the shelf to the buyer due to a low price, which makes a product become a possible fashion for purchase even though it is truly not needed outside the location of where it originates or has its true value. Additionally, when a product leaves the store at a price lower than its worth, the cost of extracting the product from our planet, the cost of moving it to the store and the cost of paying all workers involved in bringing the product to market must not add up to more than the total price that the product is finally sold for. However, extraction costs, transportation costs, and worker's wages for bringing the product to the public do not go down just because the price of the final offering goes down. Where, then does the extra currency come from to pay all those involved in bringing the below-market price product or service to market? This system then must fail and must cause more to be extracted, perhaps far afield, to make up the difference. And the true negative of such a system is that our planet is gouged for more and more in a mad massacre to keep the currency flowing, even when such products are not at all needed by the public at the time they are purchased.

On the other hand, if less products and services exist than demand warrants, a number of competing consumers will fight for what is available, and only those who are stronger will survive while weaker populations of groups of people will be sacrificed. This leads to anger, fear, illness, death, violence, terrorism and war. Economic breakdown therefore, showing a separation in man's marketplace from the system in place from time immemorial of a planetary provisioning principle for all in accordance to the true need of all life here, as discussed in previous chapters in examination of the Gaia Hypothesis, is truly a breakdown of the whole Earth system – every organic cycle involved – and a possibility of a future of lack and calamity and darkness and even apocalypse becomes very possible.

The definition of economy, to be thrifty, to waste little and to save precious resources for future generations to come, does not sit well with a marketplace run amuck with gluts of goods and services sitting on shelves that then are not valuable to the public and become waste of our collective resources, with each and every one of those when in proper location and cycling patterning, is precious to life here. This then leads to a feeling among men that our planet is of less value overall and a lack of care develops in the prevalence of thought that it is okay to extract so much and waste so much without care. Without love of our home, our home also will become unloving and we as people and certainly sensitive animal life will feel unloved. Then lives become less valuable.

Further, when one considers a stock market economy, one in which goods and services are in constant production and businesses are constantly receiving investment monies even when not needed or are in excess of what those businesses can truly use to sustain a production line, without consideration, one must also consider the system itself, one that manifests a long-entrenched reality possibly antithetical to the Earth's own sowing and reaping systems, work and reward systems, that then creates a reality of non-ending supply and then need for luxury instead of plain or true life choices. What the true model would be without a stock pile mentality, whether one needed more of certain things in advance while others might need more at other times or other places, is anyone's guess. However, a stock market mentality, of exchanging in advance, and then realizing or creating a need to match the advance decision – whether true or untrue to demand of consumers – means a certain few – in just one business venture and there are so many millions, aren't there – determine our market choices (and many Earth choices) which might be very different products available from our planet than might have been there had individuals kept their own innate power to choose their life everyday.

CHAPTER FIVE

MINI-SYSTEMS OF MAN

That natural cycles of our planet are always perfect
and function in time (movement) and spatial patterns
(moving through area or location). These elemental
gifts given to us from our father, ranging from things
such as nitrogen and methane and hydrogen and
proteins, stream down to us to sustain and develop
us, and course through certain terrains and strata
and regions of our planet. They flow together with
our land in a harmonic path according to a single
calendar, beginning at number one and ending 1000

years later, intertwined in mathematical perfection with each other to together culminate at the end of each 1000 year cycle in one unified occurrence. For example, the Earth water system courses through our airways, waterways and land, coming down as rain, down into the ground into our underground water table, coursing through all streams, rivers and lakes and also cycling though the seas and oceans. The course of this cycle of water shows a pattern designed each day to maintain each molecule to complete its cycle at the end of each 1000 year period, all in perfection with the need of all other sustaining elements and in harmony with the needs of all life.

The pattern of man, however, in contrast to that of animal life or plant life or the patterns of elemental cycling, is one in tragedy, disarray and discordance. While we know that Earth systems and life forms must work and receive reward as they interrelate with one another and help sustain each other while at the same time rewarding those working with happiness and community at the end of each working cycle, man's cycling patterns, prove to work otherwise, with selfishness and greed ruling, causing many systems which are affected by the action of man to suffer. And that leads to disruption of the perfect majesty of our planet. In this day of war, racism, poverty, deforestation, pollution and rampant consumerism contrasted against populations with no hope, dependent upon charity, we see our fellows devouring our planet quickly and ravenously without regard to future generations of people, animals and plants, or God himself who loves us and needs to know we want to survive.

CHAPTER SIX

STOCK MARKET SYSTEM WORKING WITHIN EARTH SYSTEM

The stock market represents an imperfect system because it hurts life due to its nature of stockpiling sustaining natural resources for the benefit of companies without oversight who take often from far-off locations, probably paying not at all the true cost of those resources and their worth to the Earth had they stayed properly in their inherent locations, leaving such locations with traumatic loss of sustenance. Once those stock piles are removed they are left sitting elsewhere waiting to be used to please a not-mathematically-sound market system that places future need (as shares of companies are sold which money is needed for authenticating the system to buy these stockpiles) that may not be valid above true current needs. This purchase against future need in order to justify taking in money in advance of actually producing a product so that pocketbooks can be brimming goes against the Gaia philosophy and may inhibit Earth cycling which in this author's minds works more along the lines of a just-in-time marketplace where needs are filled as they are needed and not in advance for some that then would mean another goes wanting.

To waste parts of the planet, so that a profit can be made, which then transfers some forms of life and the living purpose of those life forms and their potential to the decisions of stock marketeers earning a profit and offering those resources for completely different than the inherent purposes to a far-off population not in majority of cases intended to have those things takes away the stolen resources from functioning within their original community and in connectivity with all life there originally acting together in harmony as a system and as originally imagined. This means that the divine purpose of our planet in certain locations is extracted and subverted, which leads to pain and suffering, unbelievable feelings of loss and disarray, disharmony and disease. Those missing pieces then, and the ones that are left behind in their locations, may take on a new purpose or a strange aberrated purpose, apart from each other, in the wrong composition and connectivity and controlled by the wrong hands. These are within the family of elements, still perhaps cycling and having their divine purpose as their innate nature dictates, but not located properly and considered possibly a disorder aberrantly hurting part of the Earth. Instead of being a part of the natural sustenance of the whole Earth purpose and life, forced into a new purpose, perhaps antithetical to the original purpose, the parts in a small way change the intention of the Earth, in some ways perhaps bringing that true purpose to the new location and mission and at the same time not completely attuned to its purpose in a perfect way. Ultimately then, the whole Earth has to adjust to a dual functioning ideology where parts of the planet work together, but not as neighbors and therefore with delayed action and response and then next action and response, while also at the same time taking on new purposes controlled by those who took control of the removed pieces and then causing a dual reality back at home in the original location. Then, the planet may come to experience in place of sublime fluidity and confluence a more angular geometry and mathematical standpoint with thinking coming into being that is more intellectual and less fluid.

When profiteers of Earthly functioning cause parts of the planet meant for purity of purpose in sustenance of life to be wasted to falsely satisfy lives of miniscule minorities in comparison to the numbers meant to be helped, and an important and integral part of the whole being is wasted and forced to act in added capacities, within the planetary spirit new emotional and thoughtful cadences can develop: sadness, loss, anxiety — and these new additions to original planetary composition affection all physical and emotional health on Earth. Further, while such feelings that affect the whole and its functioning occur, the planet must somehow over-compensate for all negative and unbalanced and unjust impacts that have occurred and that are occurring while still finding ways to heal the disturbance and bring back harmony and still continuing to meet each current need for sustenance of life of the whole – adding a new function to the whole that was not there originally and that taxes the planet against its allotted daily energy. In order for these adjustments to work, a carefully configured healing plan comes into being, creating a new added cycle of life – a new planetary cycle, carried out every day side by side with the planet carbon cycle and hydrological cycle and nitrogen cycle, to name just three – so that the original harmonies of all cycles can function together as best possible harmony available. This author believes that in the places where the most suffering on Earth exists, the worst examples of the above-described disturbances can be found. It is from those locations and the points of departure of things meant to stay permanently that the original perfection of a system broke down.

As the stock market sells more and more value or profit of businesses and those values of businesses keep changing hands, more and more people join a group owning interest in a company and then more and more profit must arise than is perhaps innate to true demand of the enterprise in order to compensate the need of all those now having interest in the business. When one studies this image carefully, however, one sees how the original resources of the planet, now removed into the business marketplace system, continue to act as they would if they had been kept originally in their sacred locations. The people, and even animals, living near the business, frequent these enterprises, and shopping becomes the national pastime in so many locations, because just as life seeks sustenance and love from the planet, the same thing then occurs as people step into the hotels and restaurants and shops seeking sustenance there. However, the made products in most cases do not match the healthiest choices for man and animal and vegetation, climate and land. That is why even though the marketplace is one of the in some ways most fun and joyful aspects of life here, it also holds an onus of later disease and disharmony as the fulfillment offered by these things is not a perfect healthful response to our inner truth, changing our insides away from a once inner perfection.

DO STOCK MARKET PHILOSOPHIES LIMIT THE ENDLESS CREATIVE WEALTH INHERENT TO LIFE ON EARTH

The stock market is an upsetting phenomenon on Earth. What is upsetting about the stock market is that it presents a strict reality of choice of consumers with rigid borders, taking many aspects and features of the Earth and narrowly defining them into purposes imagined by the stock market architects. A life without such rigidly drawn realities of choice would be one completely differing from stock market constructionists which today govern most cultures in terms of the choices life offers us. In fact, one cannot know and cannot imagine what life on Earth would be like if there were no stock market. A good lesson in every schoolroom would result if professors were to ask students what they would imagine their lives to be if no stock market and all it truly entailed existed. If teachers guiding our children from their innocent early imaginings to the more complex thinking adulthood asked their students to relate their beliefs of what life would be like without the stock market system, a compendium of thinking and perhaps hope and dream would develop showing what idyllic lifestyles could be realized if such possibility were available to the true need in innocent life.

This author believes that life in complex societies, imagine without the complex social and financial machine of stock market-money changing among millions if not trillions of hands daily, would be dramatically different if such profiteering from simply putting money in different places at all times and then expecting profit from each transaction did not exist. Imagine how this system adversely affects the Earth system, where our needs and wants might be paid for by exercise of our daily output of work, but where, certainly, an extra added profit for each action taken during our work day, is not possible for addition – otherwise wouldn't our planet be as broke as the federal budget? People involved in this way of thinking, that they deserve not just their daily allotment among all people and other life here, and somehow in accordance to their nature and daily output here, but also deserve profit in addition, which takes from another, cause the planet to lose its resources and its wealth and its ability not just to mundanely provide but also to be fruitful and multiply a continuous round of miraclousness with is our privilege within a world that can provide such when in health.

Another consideration of stock market economies is that businesses using the stock market exist side by side with businesses that do not. One must consider the ramifications of a dual system and the pros and cons of that and how the two prevailing systems reflect what now also occurs within the other cycles of the planet, interwoven within all natural cycling. One aspect of all business is called marketing and market research, a phenomenon wherein business leaders study their business ideas' chances of success. Before any successful endeavor is embarked upon, for example, in many cases a market is first studied and researched to see in advance the viability of the proposed products and/or services a business will bring forth. This means that inherent in our marketplace is an amount of forecasting the future and then in some what steering it forth. This mentality adds a new dimension to the idea of natural resources being removed from their most desired and sacred location with a dilution of original purpose and addition of another or many other purposes away from their most sacred spots and then with the added burden that a future has been developed for the resources along a course designed by many others, whose thinking and temperaments are diverse. Additionally, the ability of Mother Nature to transform and accommodate and create things new becomes more limited as her resources become narrowly defined in certain structured business models. Without this constraint, all life on Earth would be left to imagine and then manifest chosen offerings and experiences to the marketplace of their most innate need and the need of their loved ones from perhaps millions more of different possibilities.

If the above model were to change, a new spectrum of creative thought and a new type of marketplace would be available – allowing a renaissance to flourish in many ways. Then, instead of a dual system of wealthy over-indulged and over-privileged, yet restricting business models having more control than simpler smaller neighborhood businesses that more truly reflect the community standards and buying choices and lifestyle needs and mindset, the world could become one again, in a true circular, all-inclusive, yet diverse, system broken down. What might be possible to conceive is that men would possibly become engaged in a new type of day-to-day marketplace, which might in some ways take advantage of the old models which foster friendship and communication across many boundaries but in the new model with a different creative goal. This author concludes that developing consumer need in advance for life here, well before many people are even ready to start shopping, creates empty lives and unhappiness because true resources that the Earth would perhaps prefer to offer are short-circuited.

A stock market economy represents a system of man antithetical to the nature of the Gaia Hypothesis. The opposite would be a playing field of small, medium and large business – all chances equal – taking their places among each other and united in a synchronized and harmonic marketplace truly serving the brotherhood of man. So many less people would need unemployment monies, would need workman's compensation, would need social assistance and disability income, would need to worry about minimum wage jobs that do not meet the true expense and cost of living, which are so heightened due to the movement of natural resources away from their perfect and sacred location where their elemental nature works at its truest and best potential, not removed to a spot chosen by man to satisfy a singular need. This cycle costs the Earth much in wealth meant for sustenance of all life and we do all then suffer poverty and removal from all miracles once available to us. It is then that mankind's innate need to be creative and in creative harmony with others is short-changed. What is a second set of cycling, not within planet and within the cycling patterns of our elements and resources, but on top of the ground, where we set up our homes and workplaces, wherein man might have set up a marketplace and home life pattern more aligned with the Gaia Hypothesis laws that would have allowed governance of our choices at home to equal harmonic forms of exchange in personal and public spheres that would have built a well-woven quilt of ebbing and flowing friendship and brotherhood in all layers of exchange possible, is the true miraculous potential available if man chose to have it.

The benefit to such a system more truly mirroring the true Earth plan is that warlike and terroristic feelings would not be prevalent as people from every age and gender and ethnic background and culture and class would join the marketplace successfully with welcome and not shut doors with a whole new feeling among people being possible. What we feel now when we join the marketplace as employers or employees is worry, agitation and immense negativity due to competitive divisive factors prevailing, separating neighbors family and friends. With huge homogenous stock market companies taking so much of the share of income that the consuming public has to offer, in addition, the quality of life of those consumers becomes so pared down by the similarity of choice available since so much of the marketplace is governed by the minds of so few men. With a multiplicity of creative thought governing the market, with all men able to participate, as an example different from that current state, more would be available each day to consider a part of life and a part of experience than the same choices day after day and year after year. Because of that state of affairs, a set of classes of people, so dissatisfied with life's experiencial offerings, delve into alternative lifestyles seen as negative that are then ruined by the development of problems associated with those individuals who see their reputations in their communities lowered. This downturn of some names over others leads to hostility just as the competitive nature of becoming a part of the workplace – so difficult to enter what should be so easy – creates a whole societal system deviating away from the gentle mind and toward the aggressive.

Another consideration of stock market versus non-stock market mentalities is how our geography is determined by what happens on Wall Street. Wall Street creates a certain way of thinking that then leads to a physical reality in terms of many environmental factors that with so much money and natural resource involved seems to take over every aspect of life. Spreading out from the stock market are road maps and ways feeding into cities and towns and suburbs and country sides. Those living in far-off rural environments may have physical geographical beauty and freedom from constraint, but at the same time by virtue of escaping the heavily-laden stock market leadership, live in poverty away from the marketplaces and oftentimes in the areas where the natural resources are taken so that the stock markets can prevail. The geographical ugliness of certain areas of the world is due to a congestion and conglomeration of many industrial enterprises and ways of thinking as well as technological processes that put a heavy burden in one small location which in addition to so much processing taking place there takes away from more isolated areas that need their terrain at home and not necessarily a part of the system developed elsewhere. Also, the system in place becomes an integral part of the Earth's natural cycling, as the parts of these do come from the natural environment. This then means the Earth must compensate for so many of its natural resources and elements a running a part of a very large and complex process in a contrast different from their original intent, away from their original location, and then not fending for and caring for the original whole that operated and was designed in a specific way. This problem is the major challenge the Earth faces insofar as sustainability, taking away our own health to feed a marketplace that is not healthy for us to injest. The environments suffering as they create too much that is unhealthy and feed the populations of animal man climate and vegetation what is unhealthy and then take so much of what we have that is available for cleaning and maintaining hygiene. If there were no stock markets, exchange between people and our relationship to our planet and all life here as a whole might be completely different, hopefully more in truth relativity to the natural of our truth as a planet and its original nature which is a loving nature and not an unhealthy nature.

Finally, without stock markets, which in essence by definition mean a stock-pilling mentality in advance of need of such commodities, there would be no taking from others who at any given moment might need some of the things that were taken. There would not be need for war between otherwise civilized populations, this author believes, if such stock-piling mentality were not to exist.

CHAPTER EIGHT

DEBT

Being in debt is always a bad thing. Man's mini-systems coursing through the planet along with its natural elemental flows are taking too much from the whole. As a whole, therefore, mankind is in debt. And where are we financially and in terms of leading truly healthy and fruitful lives that are unencumbered by painful knowledge that we lack a good future due to owing something back to the past? And what is it we can do in order to bring health back to our home? The new choice and decision that must first be made and then put forth is to no longer put our own need in front of the need of our shared home the Earth. And to pay back old debts, even if they are not personally our own and perhaps belong to a neighbor. By simply deciding to on a daily basis give a gift of fresh clean water, say, to wild life, who might at present be surviving with only dirty salty ocean water, we enhance our own lives in so many ways, and our health and land and planet and our future. By making other similar choices, for example, to choose to help each month a senior or a senior center, in this author's opinion, we increase our wealth by large measure and our personal fortunes each day against the old bad debt.

THE GAIA HYPOTHESIS

SECTION II

THE INDIVIDUAL AND THE GROUP

LIFE ON EARTH /
THE INDIVIDUAL
AND THE GROUP

The dichotomy we speak of in regard to man's versus animals' long-embedded contradictory and dualistic behaviors must be analyzed if one wants to truly understand why there is dissension and long-standing conflict on Earth. The dichotomy of being is evidenced in the differences seen in action, thought and communication of animals, which act and live instinctively and innately, entwined with the planet, guided by it and guiding it back, and man, who acts and lives theoretically, knowing natural living but choosing to understand it from afar, but not be within it. AIso, while man may be guided by the planet's loving, living self, he responds often times with cruel actions, thoughts and words involving murder of both animals and plants. Both of these methods - the natural unfolding of animals from within our innate planetary truths and the dualistic approach of man, knowing unfolding but choosing to take turns away into what would not naturally unfold, occur always at the same time, and both together lead to contradictions in planetary mood and thinking. This is because among animal and plant life, an intuitive "tropism," acting, thinking and communicative behavioral set, are evidenced, because the animals and plants synchronously act and react together as part of the same being along with our bigger world around them. However, in man - where a more analytical and theoretical style of thinking, acting and speaking prevails - a way has evolved, perhaps outside of tropism, that sets him apart and he remains separated to some degree from the natural planet. Animals cannot be separated. Man's thinking, however, is formed from an ancient trend and now prevails as his natural way culled in the modern sense from his family and their history and also from the school room, which create behaviors in man learned from outside sources to him, not just from his innate being, as is the case with animals. These outside, societal forces have shaped man throughout history. And that is the separation clearly stated; man fills his intelligent intuitive mind with knowledge from outside of himself instead of believing that he has his own innate knowledge to draw upon. From this phenomenon we have many many people who act, think and speak alike. We might as men and women show something different in our lives - the words, thoughts, deeds unique to each individual - if man culled more from his natural soul which bears many unique gifts and talents from man to man to offer from. And we might be more tightly knit into nature had we not created an evolutionary path separate from the natural world. This author believes that the separation of man has led to disease and war and all the negative phenomenon on our planet that a Gaia follower would deem unhealthy.

The separation of man has been in place since the flood of Noah, when men experienced many behavioral changes. This was when man chose to start sacrificing animals and eating them. Therefore, in the beginning, separate behaviors seen in man may have stemmed from experiencing catastrophe, e.g., the traumatic flooding of that time. In the distant past, when men lived as one with all natural life, men were similar to animals and simply unfolded while connected to all of nature. However, as men evolved, through catastrophe, they came into an evolution where men are now obliged and expected to live as "society" dictates, in a separated manner from what dictates might come from the natural world working vis a vis man's own innate soul. These new expectations involve telling people what is right to eat and drink, what are the right behaviors to set in motion to earn your living, what is the correct way to choose your husband or wife, how one must act in public, how one must keep up a home, and the list might go on. Man would not give up these tenets and the world built upon them for anything. But the beliefs underpinning much of man's civilized world may be proven in some ways to be evil. That is because his societies are built on killing and a selfish form of sustenance over and above a caring form meant for the whole of man if he were united with his brethren and the planet wholly. Man tends to analyze the world and then by himself or with a chosen few decide what his place is within it and what he might earn from it, while animals' innate nature and instinctual actions cause their more complete immersion into the planetary cycles in a way that is best for Earth's natural needs, causing animals to act and react naturally with the planet as it evolves, and they evolve with it, and always staying within their rightful place. The planet then chooses things for them while man tries to choose things for himself. This explains why man is separated from the natural world and functions in a way through a barrier to it called technology. From the separated methods of animal versus human behavior we see evidence in myriad ways that the two forms of behaving do not coalesce well. That is because the evolution of animals and the natural Earth may be too large a degree different from the continued evolution of man.

One has to wonder why man chooses and has chosen throughout history to learn and think about and, further, to sometimes deeply study, the meaning of life and in many cases to grasp it, while at the same time choosing to act in his and her personal life discordantly from the truths learned. Through the study of subjects stemming from school book threads, such as mathematics and physics and psychology and reason and philosophy and religion, man learns many truths of our divine nature and the divine nature of all interconnected life on Earth, but at the same time in many cases he does not use his or her advanced learning to live a better life more aligned with true

Earth philosophy and law. And he chooses to act not as the Earth, our home, needs him to act. Many people fight Gaia's philosophy that the Earth is alive and man has a true role within that philosophy that is probably very different from the truth of the path he has instead chosen. However, while somehow adjoined to this connected life, man is also satisfactorily turned to the side of it. Somehow, even with all of his learning and philosophical knowledge, he has chosen to know things from afar, living disconnected from planetary law, in fact breaking its common tenets, with his choices and decisions favoring a path apart from the intuitive and innate among us. Indeed, in man's willful disregard of the natural world as he plunders forests and fields and hurts animals and their habitats, he chooses to know the truth of Earth life, yet to deviate from it in his daily activities. In fact, most men could be called deviants. This dichotomy of having a thirst for knowledge and then a pursuit of knowledge and having depth and intelligence enough to learn truth through this pursuit while at the same time choosing a deviant path is heartbreaking. And one can find example after example of the truth of this foregoing statement.

There are so many examples of man's life - historically and in the modern ways - showing his disturbing choice to know life and at the same time to want to conquer it and plunder it. While learning biology he came to see the value of all life and the reliance of all life upon all other life while the daily sowing and reaping of work and reward undertaken by all life, a natural planetary regulatory system keeping all life interconnectedly healthy and stable, takes place. However, even while understanding this, man chose throughout history to operate apart from his role in the interconnected systematic working and rewarding reality and to come to work for himself as a closed partner separate and apart from the other partners of our interconnected life. From that decision came a selfish disregard for the Earth system of life connectivity and its need to sow and reap together and share work and reward together as one unified being. Instead, turning to a more self-oriented way - sowing separately for oneself - and then, one assumes, reaping alone – man chose a deviation from the natural Earth system and caused disruption of the planet's true method of functioning in regard to sowing work to create sustenance for all life.

One example of this dichotomy is seen through man's theories that have developed about vitamins. For example, when men began to try to improve brain function through the ingesting of certain vitamins, such as fish oil capsules, those doing this may have erred, because it seems impossible that one would be rewarded by investing in something that came from a killed animal. This author believes more in intuitive methods of healing, however, from natural processes of the Earth, maybe learned from the study of animal behavior and/or plant life activity. The reason this author feels this way is that the method of ingesting fish oil as a remedy probably developed from separated thinking and not innate thinking.

In writing this book, this author is aiming to take an intuitive approach and let go of separated thinking - at least for the duration of this essay. Some of the book's propositions may therefore seem odd or out-of-the-ordinary, but in many cases the truth of even strange-seeming theories can be found. The strangeness of some of the chapters of this book comes from trying to think innately and intuitively and not just from book knowledge. We are not used to that path but it helps to try it when one wants to see some truths in life that are often overlooked.

In thinking of using parts of fish to heal with, for example, this author believes it will not work. On the other hand, this author's intuitive self believes that if fish were left free to swim and multiply and be prosperous, always in their own habitat, just as we are free to maintain the inalienable right to have a home and freedom therein and thereabouts, just the act of their swimming and following their natural behavioral course would lead - this author believes - to healthy brain function among other life forms included with the underwater aquatic life, without the need for ingesting fish oil. There may even be empirical evidence culminating from research studies of oceanic animal life that supports this theory that healthy behaviorally-wealthy aquatic animal life is a more healthful tonic to our thinking mechanisms and brain than say investing in fish oil would be. These studies point out that fish in their migratory activities directly affect nutrients that are related to temporal activity in a general, overall sense, because one of the most important behaviors of living fish is the transport of ocean, lake and sea nutrients from one area to another in a never-ending manner. And the nutrients directly involved, as stated above, relate to the temporal. This active pathway fish travel along leads to oxygen rich water with plant life in good health in the locations affected. These end results cause other aquatic life and life on land to prosper too. That's because we are all interconnected through the elemental water cycle traveling throughout our planet in all of its parts, touching all of us. That is why fish, left to roam as part of the water cycle, which is embedded within every aspect of our ambient and un-ambient world, bring health through their own innate behavior interacting rightly with our planet and it interacting rightly with them, to every one of us. If, on the other hand, there developed over-fishing in oceanic or lake or sea areas, and certain area fish populations were adversely impacted (maybe sometimes for the gathering of fish oil!), then what has been shown to happen next is a loss of healthy watery vegetation in those spots. This creation of unhealthy water habitats can adversely affect all of us. Later, more fish will die with the loss of the first set and then even later there will be no nutrient transporting activity. This leads to the development of what are called dead zones, where there is no oxygen any longer, where once oxygen-abundant areas became ridden with life having died there and then having become dead zones where life cannot be sustained because there is not enough oxygen in those places in the ocean. The ocean when healthy can be thought of as a wondrous, magical place, just, say, like a forest is special to us, full to the brim with myriad life active throughout the day and night creating only good for our world. This good is not just for the watery world a lone but for all of us. That is because the entire ocean and all of its great activity, as stated above, is also apart of the water cycle embedded into our planet, cycling not just throughout the ocean but in lakes and streams and underground waterways and then also as part of the rain cycle throughout the trees and clouds. One can see how this healthy magical happening helps humans through the loving nature of aquatic life prospering their gifts to us in a natural way always. If even one murder occurs in the ocean then much is lost. In regard to the specifics of fish life, we know that fish are involved in temporal nutrient transporting activity and good chemistry of nutrients flourishing (among them oxygen), which from the ocean which is vast (bigger than a fish oil tablet), leads to healthy brain function outside among man. Therefore, if fish are healthy, exercising and moving well in their share of water, our lives too will be healthier because into the cloud cover above us the nutrient-rich molecules from the waterways rise. This occurs naturally in our planet because ocean water and molecules are a part of the planet's water cycle - which includes the fish transporting activities - and then the elevating of nutritious molecules rising to a formed marine layer above and then into the cloud cover everywhere and then down into the land as rain gives us nutrient-rich moist H20 to keep us active and healthy. This also leads to prosperity of all vegetation growing which is close to man's food sources and oxygen cycles. Therefore, man becomes directly a part of the nutrient transport wealth when he breathes in healthy oxygen and partakes of food from Earth vegetation. Put simply, human life entwines innately with this cycle through breathing and the nutrient-rich molecules in the atmosphere become a part of us, to the benefit of our health, everywhere, as we simply breathe each day.

Another way to look at the connection between fish (and all life) is to analyze breathing. Every living being breathes, animals, plants and humans. This is why we are alive as Gaia states it. we all breathe in a combination of oxygen mixed with water (except for plants which breathe in and out in an opposite way from man and animals). Together, breathing in and out, man and fish are connected and all life is connected. This happens through the spirit contained within our planetary atmosphere. Therefore, we are all connected, through our thousands and the animals' and plants' many thousands, of breaths all mingled together in the surrounding ethos and biosphere. From such a phenomenon we feel each other and know each other very well. It correlates then that as all life breathes together they become through the spirit which surrounds us all, connected. Explained in another way, the very motion of constant breathing in and out of all life together, eternally, daily, during every minute, leads to a great interconnection that most people may not realize. Therefore the goal of maintaining a healthy living planet among itself and all its beings within it, the health of all life together, if realized, would lead to all life together staying, and being allowed to stay, healthy, because - as we breathe in together and then breathe out - we share our individual health with - through the breathing aspect – multitudes of lives of the whole. This sharing of breath and health together creates a uniform multiple insurmountable form of great health expressed everywhere. If one person ever felt short of breath, then, the unified sharing together of breathing might straighten him or her right up, but that level of help to strengthen that person may be dependent upon the level of health available on the planet in an overall way at the time the illness appears. Therefore, in order to stay healthy on our planet, one must pray for and work toward a resulting good and great and even absolute health of all life, including fish, whose exercise as part of the water cycle affects us, just as other animals' activities affect us and plants' photosynthesis activities and breathing in and out activities affects us. A dead animal creates a loss in our living planet's overall oxygenation and leaves us as a whole a living planet less alive. And an ecosystem full of dead zones is antithetical to our survival.

A testimony to the importance of multitudes of breathing beings - all alive - to our survival comes to us when we consider desert terrains. In those areas, soil is inhospitable to growth of vegetation and to sustenance of all life. That is because of the loss of oxygen in desert climates. The reason goes back to the Gaia hypothesis that our Earth is alive and must therefore live; but that means flows of oxygen between people, animals and plants must dominate each ecosystem. If there is a desert area with very little life that is because healthy breathing animal life cannot prosper there and there is a loss of living beings in the area. This affects the whole world and all of us. And without vegetation in those areas, that need the oxygen cycles as much as animals and humans do everywhere, the winds coursing through desert terrains without the stabilizing vegetation to block undue wind speeds causes desert areas to become even more terrifying. And with these strong winds the desert ecologies grow and expand into surrounding areas, and then a cycle of expanding continues outward, engulfing more terrain into the inhospitable desert. This is a terrifying calamitous series of happenings on a planet that must stay alive. Therefore, in the agenda of thinking environmentalists, knowledge of the advancing desert landscapes must be considered. The wildlife that does live in these places, perhaps burrowed under the soil, must be taken into account, because something living can heal even an inhospitable area, while dead parts with no oxygen cannot help any healing trend.

There is even another benefit to praying for a completely healthy planet with all forms hoped to be effectively healthy and the whole Earth also prayed to be in its utmost possible greatest health:that benefit is that in perfect health, the Earth can manifest its perfect life plan, along with the perfect health within it of plants, animals and man also being very likely to succeed with a resulting more close to perfect and truthful individual plan per each man and truthful plan among other life forms also prospering. And again, these individual destinies would match up perfectly with the overall perfect life purpose of the whole living planet. According to Gaia, this "alive" planet is in essence part of our bodies and the bodies of plants and animals, all connected together as part of Gaia's living Earth belief system, which as an underpinning, states: when all life in its many myriad forms is healthy, we will by natural connectivity to each other be healthy and vibrantly healthy throughout our connection together of many healthy beings. It is of utmost importance then that man stop hurting the planet's other life forms in order to stay healthy himself. That is because the life plan of our planet somehow is related to living, breathing, being alive and that plan works through connectivity not separation. Man is in truth hurting himself when he kills. Think of a world with complete health of our biosphere (all life on earth makes up the biosphere). All healthy activities, both unconsciously performed like taking in breath, seeing, smelling and hearing, and consciously performed tasks like doing business with a patron - all in multitudinous amounts - make up a living system - our biosphere, and these activities must work toward keeping living beings alive in order for our world to function rightly. We could become a continuously united healthy being, and this is where Gaia's outlook prevails, all connected to a universal health of all life forms, through sowing and reaping, keeping themselves and others alive. Unfortunately, however, on a scale of measure, the health of all of us right now, including plant life and animals and ocean life, does not make up a healthy whole. There are too many men and women either killing or, if not directly responsible, participating in enjoying a life based on killing. We are more limited now, therefore, with our waters not truly healthy but polluted, parts of our atmosphere not truly healthy but full of gas emissions, and part of our land not truly healthy but filled to the brim with landfill garbage and waste. We need very much right now to correct that. The mingling of all of our souls through the processes of breathing and smelling and hearing and seeing and tasting and touching creates a world of complete interconnectedness that cannot change. And if so many lives are dying each day - as we see that happening among plant and animal life and human life - we will only keep building as we have been building for a long time, a suicide pact and death sequence for our own lives. This comes from the murderous activities man does participate in to nourish and better himself.

To combat this, this author came up with a plan of her own contribution to helping the opposite of that sequence occur in her life. The plan involved forming a charity benefiting the Earth desert ecologies named Monarch Butterfly Land Saving Society, its goal to stimulate pollinator and habitat builder activity among unhealthy animals in order to revive them and their natural work and natural life purpose so that greater levels of pollination and habitat-building would occur among them, helping to heal them and their native ecosystems. What happened among the animals and people and other life forms in the places where the work transpired was a greater health in the ecosystems impacted. The result of the effort so far was that in the areas affected, all health did improve. And then here in the United States at home, health of the participants also went from being at a low point to resounding amazingly because, even though at times the work was being performed far afield, health at home was somehow interwoven into the transpiring of the whole series of events of the charity's work, connected to the burgeoning greatened health in the field. Anyone desirous of great health should tend to our planet's other life forms generously and then see a miracle at home. And it should be noted that in the areas where Monarch Butterfly prevailed and helped animal life and a number of plants, the life of children and adults as a result but not through a direct intervention occurred. This proved that helping one aspect of an ecosystem absolutely did also help another.

Gaia thinking involves a belief that the Earth is a living being as much as its individual parts are. This belief is supported by the above line of thought. To kill on a planet that is "alive" is a contradiction between the divine purpose of Earth - to support itself and its life, all living - and man's desire to kill these things - are completely contradictory. For example, why is man killing all of the forests! Why is deforestation so rampant! Why are so many animals extinct and continually murdered! These questions should not go unheard on a planet that exists to be alive and support life. Being that the earth is alive, one can believe that if one part of the living being is killed so that another part can partake of that part, it would be wrong karmically. And since man's society from the days of time immemorial has acted in this way, whole societies of men and women must suffer from these wrongful acts. That is because a part and piece of individual life as connected to the whole Earth life are being killed from early days to the modern time, and not only individual pieces are killed but also a part of the whole Earth being is being killed, all for servicing the benefit of another living being. The whole Earth being could never tolerate that activity. Also holding forth is the idea that if, instead of killing something to have its dead parts service you, you were to let the other being live, that being may service you in even greater measure if it were left living. (Again, examples of fish life prevailing for a healthy benefit to all Earth life is supportive of this claim.)

Another example of man taking away life to prosper his own life is evidenced in his behavior towards cows and his decision to eat cows. The cow meat, most men feel, brings health to children and adults. A diet brimming with protein, it is believed, sustains health. However, as mentioned above, it is hard to imagine how killing could on our planet – a living system - improve life. Additionally, when even one cow's life is taken, the amount of prosperity that one cow would normally bring to the Earth is lost. For example, when cows graze, six to nine hours each day, taking in pasture fodder and then ruminating it, this pollinating and habitat-enhancing procreative activity shows that cows have a large investment in our land and even own large acreage of pasture ecosystems. This taking in of fodder is a far cry than just eating and nourishing the cow. Instead, the cow is working on nourishing the land and sustaining an ecosystem. The processes that cows undertake daily and continuously contributes to the health of land for the purpose of it being sustained as biodiverse, healthy for other animals to co-habit, and also enriches places with nutrient cycling which the cows inner processes of chewing cud and ruminating contribute to. When even one cow is lost then tens of thousands of procreative pollination and habitat-building activities each year for pastures is also lost. Again, as shown with fish, our planet, needing living beings like cows to aid large ecosystems for so many animal lives and engender growing healthful forage, is made fulfilled only when cows are living, creating so much for so many, than when they are killed and taken away from this vital role. In the place of the living cows, probably more dead zones develop.

Another very important reason why it is wrong to kill life on Earth is because cows, for example, have a long history tending to pasture lands in the manor talked of above, and this is not considered when man decides to wield his weapons. For example, a whole lineage of each cows' family, also having for lengthy days tended to the same pastures within which the newest generations now work, show that cows' grazing and ruminating activities in the pastures, for more than 10 hours every day, going back through cow family lineages for centuries, are evidence that cows own the land they have through the centuries built and that their ancestors and young own the land,

and that it prospers perfectly, even magically, through the long decades, from only their tending. Taking even one animal out of this amazing life-sustaining ecosystem is criminal and divides the animal from a divine inheritance.

Additionally, one must consider the life history of fish families before one would ever kill one for a misguided and misinformed purpose. For example, fish have been swimming the Earth for 450 million years. These animals, now present, come from some of the oldest life forms of our planet, maintaining in their souls a precious historic knowledge of ocean, stream, lake and aquifer and, also, much of Earth calendar events throughout history. The knowledge transfer to newer generations is valuable to all underwater life, procreating, pollinating and habitat-building, under the waters' surface, so essential in the watery habitats.

This valuable knowledge builds up a compendium of knowledge that fish keep to help them know their pathway and divine purpose even in this most extreme example of a very large ecosystem, our ocean, in order to keep it vibrant, healthy, hygienic and connectively fruitful for all life on the planet, even those lives above on land. When a bevy of fishing activity occurs in one location, killing off a majority of dwellers there, as happens in the Jamaica area and the Baltic Sea, one takes away from our planet and it's living being it's inherent and innate knowledge of certain of its surroundings within the aquatic environment. That knowledge is important to keeping those habitats developing rightly and evolving and keeping the whole planet evolving rightly. The ocean is just too important as our largest ecosystem to hurt in any way.

Would we continue to kill our present and future evolution for the sake of sport?

Dualistic behaviors among animal and man now cause a dualism within the holistic truth and evolutionary path of our world which must create and sustain different populations of the planet differently and then separately. This creates a difficult reality for a planetary life based on holism. This separation between animal and man, created by man, has by now become systematic. Therefore, accepted as these behaviors are within the planetary evolution, we go forward each day with a combative purpose - man's purpose - different and antagonistic to the true planet purpose and animals' purpose to sublimely support us and our world. Man's actions indeed, most often do not support our world. And the Earth's evolution, since it must support man as much as it supports its other parts, has embedded man's antagonistic thinking into our very basic facets, and therefore there is much hardship in changing things. Since our world is holistic either one side should prevail or another. This creating and sustaining us creates and sustains murder even though we as a whole must stay alive. How can evolution support two oppositional tendencies? How did our living Earth allow man to break off from an evolutionary path with all life entwined? How is our evolution coping with that dualism? What will the future hold?

The funny thing about all this is that man's goals to better himself and his group first, before the larger set of people and other life, harmoniously, would be bettered, is that in the end a paradox must occur. This is because the goal of man is never reached by his manifold years of life acting in this way, and in the end man just becomes ill and dies. What good then are the individualistic tendencies of man throughout his decades here alive to live and prosper. Was there really as much prosperity in the end. If on the other hand man chose to prosper with a large number of others and considered all life on Earth in his natural acting, communicating and thinking decisions, he might be propelled into a totally different life, one connected to people and animals of all ages, that over the course of time would become one with every person involved. Then a greater health could be fostered between individuals because individual health might be shared within a much more prosperous system of connectivity between people. In a connected world - connected only by altruistic and loving feelings for other life on Earth - even our breathing is shared and our energy each day is shared and our altruism is shared (which then multiplies to be greater). And if one or a few members of the network fall ill, the interconnectivity of a large shared many years long connected health will prevail for that fallen soul or souls. This philosophy is based on a belief that our planet is in its true nature an extremely wealthy planet, able to provide enormous health and joy to all living beings. When one follows the truth, living a life based on the truth of our connection to each other, then the group prosperity which is not just added together but enormously multiplied, is shared and a life can be much more prosperous. This line of thinking prevails because the Earth mirrors back to us and gives us what we truly pray for. If you made efforts to change into a sharing, connected person, the Earth can come about to provide you this miracle. The sad thing is that in our current state, living in non-connected manners, we add bits and pieces of sustenance to our lives. With connectivity, however, multiplication of our gifts is the rule because then our world would lose its dualism which erodes so much of our wealth.

The way to begin a more healthy and prosperous life is to align positive individual thinking and acting and communicating behaviors with that of others - animals, plants, people - and then watch the new ideas prosper and multiply. Think of others as you move through your day and adjust antisocial behaviors. Then you too will prosper as you learn to grow altruistic connections between yourself and those others you joined. You might start by becoming charitable to those less fortunate than you and then watch as they in turn naturally give things back. This new emerging double pathway then oversees a shared new health and wealth coming into being.

Therefore, just as individuals have individual wealth, a second equity bank of joined health and prosperity will emerge as the new pathways foster additional and better modes of acting, communicating and thinking that benefit a group and not just one person. This will give birth to a completely different and new form of joint prosperity than what was there previously. The prosperity becomes even larger when you consider the outside connectivities of two newly joined souls who now also become added to the partnership as well. Those outer connections now brought in on either side may foster new alignments also. One day such a group could multiply shared wealth together that can easily over-shadow individual wealth. The saying "two heads are better than one" truly may demonstrate how wealthy a group over each un-unified individual can be. Just the daily ritual of thinking kindly of those others beneficially chosen by you to join in together with in charity allows you to build bridges and knock down walls. And what starts as mere thoughts will in time become concrete realities in your life with untold numbers joining you. With walls, health and prosperity are segregated into individual dosages and are disconnected from a whole larger reservoir that might ebb and flow naturally to sustain a larger number of lives with a different kind of mental attitude prevailing as the underpinning of the corrected thinking, all connected to the true fruit of our planet. Such a reservoir, coming from as large a group as you can imagine, offers a vast Earthly health not meant for a single individual or his worried over small dose. The single dose, indeed, coming from products or foods brought about by killing will not sustain the way an altruistic reservoir made by men and mirrored back at men many times over would. Many men, however, believe in the individualized approach only and unfortunately build large walls to hide their wealth. But at the same time the walls can close down that keep the same individual from a much greater wealth possible if the connection between that man and his home, the planet, were not severed. Additionally, when the walls are knocked down one can see that a large Earth inheritance given to men of altruistic feelings becomes available. Man can let that wealth flow if he chooses to knock down years-long walls saying that what is mine is mine alone. Also, the very nature of the reservoir is that as more people enter into the more altruistic feeling the greater the reservoir becomes. Then walls are not needed because in the end there is more to gain. However, somehow, throughout history men came to think that separate doses of prosperity added up to more for each individual than one unified whole prosperity would be in a world that is joined. In a world of separation of health and prosperity many dramatic and painful events occur in, say, one 24-hour day. That is a number probably so much higher than the natural law of our planet would allow in a connected visioning. However, man's separated life from others may have caused all those calamities we hear of in the news every day that dishearten us. The reason may simply be that everyone is paying daily for the separation through illness, injury and death because the separated dosages of prosperity are disconnected from the natural wellspring of the prosperity - our whole world - and naturally shrivel in individual doses away from others and away from natural law and flow which is always toward universalism. In a joined society, this author believes, the single reservoir of prosperity would be stronger and more able to easily solve our daily pains and ills. This author believes that accidents and illnesses and even death can be conquered by the reservoir of good if men chose to imagine it, speak of it, and act to create and maintain it. And the Earth would reward these efforts immediately.

There are solid reasons why wealth among sharing souls is exponentially greater and offers more for each individual than individual wealth when not shared or joined. The reason is that people who amass a wealth for themselves alone have a lot of resources for creating a selfish individual wealth and they take a lot in at a time to cover long periods - something akin to hoarding. The things hoarded, in general, are things not alive but dead. This hoarding takes things away from our planet's natural resources, also, that were once there every day to sustain us. People who rely on an income of more natural wealth based on their trust in the overall group and society and their place in it - as well as relying on living beings for sustenance and not dead beings - may lose some or much of their natural and divine inheritance to these hoarders. The people hurt are usually less wealthy souls who share more with others and somehow are still happier with less. That is because their wealth is not based on hoarding but a real-time tithing that comes as a natural gift as we choose to flow rightly with our planet. However, those that hoard and take in many methods of keeping wealth flowing to them increasingly take from the true perhaps many-fold inheriters of the prosperity and can cause losses of health in others. The others, in fact, do join the hoarders because over the years they had to rely upon them and even go to work for them as their employees. Then they may have not been able to inherit the true amount of wealth, health and overall prosperity that they were entitled to over a lifetime. This may have contributed to many illnesses and forms of lack and even caused death when life for much longer periods may have been possible. Indeed, this prevailing hoarders' world - turned away from the world of Gaia because it is a world made of dead zones – may have afflicted man from the time of the end of the flood of Noah, continuing on until this day. Much of that world we have so become akin and inured to depends on killing plant life and animal life to survive. And that is irregular that we have come to feel from the hoarders that to survive we must take things by killing them and then rely on killed once living things to survive. As stated above, the living plants and living animals benefit us so much more than the same numbers in death. Us choosing to survive by their death may have led to a reversal of our fortunes even with an unknown hoarder having created it, and many innocent lives may have been lost to death due to the dependence in their lives upon dead things to survive while a hoarding few have been in control. The above line of thinking shows how the wealth of our planet, and over the years this has been enormous amounts of wealth, has been squandered for very few takers who then set up enterprises to share a bit of the wealth amassed for those who might come to be hired to help that system prevail. But it is easy to see had the Earthly prosperity been left in place and had plant and animal life not been killed, how our health, wealth and prosperity would have been many fold times greater from letting the animals and plants just prosper naturally and left their non-violated by-products there as gifts for us prevail.

A man that thinks of his Earthly inheritance as separate from others' inheritances and who is not a responsible copartner with our planet and home is a man that believes in killing plants and forests and prairies and pastures and animals in order for him to bring to his own home a wealth of products and foods. How many trees and animals are killed each day just to keep one superstore running with a personal, individualized wealth beyond measure? Instead, if a co-partnership of altruistic men and women were to keep going healthy and wealthy pastures brimming with calcium from years of cow grazing and ruminating practices then they would have so many of the food products they and their children might need that would grow as by-products from cow activity for our use. Since just one cow produces 90 liters of saliva every day laden with nutrients from chewing their cud and ruminating, which then every day pours into the pastures, making these pastures vital sinks of nutrient-rich food producing places, one can see how the loss of just one cow destroys a great inheritance. Such cow-populated places are rich with nutrients for many a man to reap grown vegetation, grain, gelatin, seed and dry milk weed there easily to nourish wealthily their families. There is simply no just cause to kill even one cow when just one's daily activities bring about so much food for many to reap. The wealth for all coming from just one cow's activities is enormous. Why kill these purveyors of great and healthy food for eating the cow like cannibals in an individualized manner never thinking of the greater whole, in essence stealing our planet's population's health and wealth for the benefit of a few men who sacrifice so many of us who lose our natural inheritance?

This concept of the difference between individual wealth versus the nature of wealth when a large number are involved cooperatively is worthy of consideration. Imagine one superstore that amassed untold wealth for maybe 50 to 100 individuals. How much is taken from our planet daily to sustain that small number of individual prosperity so that consumer products and goods can continually be put forth? What if instead a large collective of individuals bought the land that those plundered from and then did not allow the plundering any longer? What if the land slowly returned back to its natural state? How many offerings from that particular regenerated wilderness area would there be for the new collective dwelling there? There might be thousands of trees, thousands more of other vegetation, nuts, fruits, grains and seeds to nourish untold thousands of animals that would take our small investment and make it the wealthiest place on Earth. That is because not only would their natural procreative gift be up and operational again but a new sense of gratitude to the new group helping each animal being reborn would prevail. The animal life would know that men saved them and, this author is sure, would in return save them back. That is Earthly karmic law operating and such law cannot be changed.

For men to agree to become different in their attitudes, changing from individualized thinking to group thinking, they might first be willing to consider their own neighborhoods as a good place to start. Why not get to know neighbors and forge a fertile ground of friendship. Communities could agree to adopt Neighborhood Watches for their street to alert members to potential crime. Or an Elderly Oversight program for caring for homebound elders could be adopted. A meal service to disabled or otherwise ill neighbors could be enacted. Being forever politically minded, Americans could think of many reasons to start neighborhood groups that then join families across many boundaries. Within such new ties that might develop many conversations that then would be in the offering would become additions to the conversation of the original group purpose. Think of the ties of friendship that could develop amid a once solidly individualized motto. From such newly fertile ground so much good can develop for group thinking.

This author believes that many individually-minded neighbors can change into group thinkers and concerned citizens by just starting the process as described above to improve their neighborhood. The group thinking that would emerge is a new pathway and in some ways that new pathway might preclude once serious hoarders into stopping such practices as they see how such activities might affect a larger group, for example, a group like their burgeoning friendly neighborhood. If you were to mingle in to your neighborhood differently and see the state of the lives of non-hoarders you may begin to feel ashamed of your actions. You may care more for a disparaged group and slowly ebb away from some degree of hoarding into a caring inclusion of others into wealth. This simple yet amazing process might build strong bridges and pathways for a new kind of group thinking to flow through. These thoughts become stronger as the Earth would reward you with a better, more truthful success in life than you would have received during the days of lonely hoarding. Additionally, change toward group thinking, speaking and acting seems very possible when one simply realizes how many more numbers of group thinkers there are on Earth as opposed to the much smaller numbers of individual thinking types. Why not make it a demand in your own thinking privately to change in any way you can to become an activist for group inclusion. Work on saving plant and forest and animal life. Join as many groups already working in these areas. Find a way to break barriers of thinking that are oppositional but that you know can be changed when a direct good foreseeable change in the individual's life that you are trying to affect would be seen easily to be improved from the breaking of the status quo.

We see clearly how animals have divine purposes here on Earth, their purpose among us to help procreate and multiply their gifts for their own groups and families and also for others such as man. They are here for their families as they reap but when they sow they share so much with others, even some far off species. To add something of your being to land and pasture or ocean and stream, and then through that activity to help a planet thrive with all life so much interconnected to thrive also, is a divine path indeed. And that animals, so talented, creating gifts for man and others every day, innately act in this manner shows plainly their divine nature and this points to a hypothesis that animals are divine. From this theory one can surmise that man too is divine. We may not believe that because our actions have sunk low indeed, that we now kill animals and ruin forests, also so full of gifts from a bio-diverse population, in order to honor our choice to thrive while others have died in order for us to feel that we can succeed. If one can imagine a world that might be here with us if man had not chosen this course of murder and plunder, one might see such a different planet. What would it look like with all animals never extinct but here among us, with forests and fields full to brimming with earthly gifts, with man not carnivorous but gentle. This author feels that the divine nature of all living beings, including man, would be shown. There might be different purposes for man than simply going to work every day for less than scrupulous others but instead working each day harmoniously with the whole of our world and for the betterment of all. That man has such great intelligence and physical prowess granted him and to not be using such gifts for divine purposes is criminal. What indeed also would be the mortality rate in a world without slaughter of animals but love for all beings among you? You might find that the prophecies of the Bible, that eternal life is available to all, would prevail. It is hard to imagine such a world, one where the purpose of man would be aligned with loving feelings and not murderous hatred shown toward other forms of life. It is hard to imagine a world without meat-eating and slaughterhouses and instead beautiful green pastures everywhere and forests fully flourishing. It is hard to imagine life eternal and life not cut short at an early age. But without choosing the rampant course we are traveling many different and wondrous events and pathways would prevail in place of the darkness we choose. What would the better world hold for us? It is hard to imagine the good and the prosperous potential available to us by simply changing a few bad habits.

A good question is how to bring back and bring out in this modern technological day the true divine nature of all life on Earth, including man. This would seem a question for the church or synagogue or mosque. However, it is in the everyday activities, thoughts and communications that such divinity should now begin to show itself. The daily routine of every man is the stomping ground for such change. And it is in every day activities that one must recognize our shared responsibility toward shining out that side of our nature and trying to imagine ways in the daily routines to live up to a different standard than what we have been living outwardly and within for eons. Some may come to realize a level of darkness in their daily lives when considering a better path. How then to move dark men's actions, thoughts and words into the light. That would be a simple way to make a myriad of great changes in each person. A simple change of substituting animals in our food to vegetables would lead over time to a lighter body that would be less dense. Meat tends to create density in our physiques while vegetables bring in light. You might even find that a body full of vegetables and not dense meat attracts some level of photosynthetic reactions to your body on a continuous basis. That would bring you into harmony with the natural world and would offer you a greater chance at overseeing a divine path emerging. Also, this form of reacting with the sunlight from within your soul might bring a wellspring of health to vegetarians.

You may think that you are enlightened and do indeed travel a divine path because you have always attended religious services. However, that opinion just underlies the fact that man has chosen a theoretical path towards his divine nature and not an innate one. To learn the truth and to even pray for truth in your life does not guarantee that you live the truthful path. In fact, many people's divided thinking is easily evidenced by their dependence on say church services while during the average days in the work week there is far wandering away in action, thought and communication from what is a divine path as may be espoused in a synagogue. This is a perfect example showing how man thirsts for divine truth but then will not live within his divinity during the remaining six days of the week when he turns away. And that is because those days are devoted to earning our daily bread, and making money, and it is in the actions, thoughts and communications associated with earning that we fail. We continue to kill animals for our food and continue to lay importance on money even often over the importance within us of friendships and family ties. This scenario depicts lives lived in darkness and not in the light.

A way to start asking for more light in your life and to try to touch onto your divine nature is to expect and value your inner realizations. Realizations that come in life are truthful gifts from a higher plateau that culminate when you have fully studied a subject or emotionally experienced a life-changing situation and then feel yourself being alit with higher thoughts and realizations meant to help you. Through realization, amazing truths about yourself and your life are revealed to you. In any situation at hand, you are then given tools to best navigate through them. Realizations can be trusted without mistake or misgiving because they bring in objective truth, not subjective emotions or hypotheses. Prayer is one of the best ways, as is meditation, and calming exercises, to bring realization into your life. Also a Godly plan, or just a plan of a good person meant for good results for yourself and others, and steadfastly sticking to that plan, can also lead to realizations coming to you of immense value. And when you begin to have realization in your life, your life will start to become one lived along with truth and not separated from truth. You will then gain assurance that the right path is the path of light, with joined thinking, and not the path of dark, where you operate for yourself alone. One important thing to note is that while you might think that living within your truthful nature and experiencing realizations that guide you along each day in a path of divinity is difficult to attain, you would be thinking wrongly. The reason is that you are already divine but through the evolution of man, you have simply decided not to acknowledge this fact. Man instead chose to be closed to inner realization of his true best nature and chance to be eternally healthy in favor of believing instead in a selfish lifestyle favoring his own need there and above the needs of others and the Earth as a whole. If one simply decided to not believe this way any longer, so much would go right in that person's life, as dreams would be fulfilled, as life's path would straighten and as more love and prosperity would enter into that life. And these things flowing to you - when you offer yourself to learn of your true nature - help your gifts not just double or triple in your destiny but multiply manifold. That is because once love is flowing, people change and become open to the beauty of existence and their own personal part of the shared life we own. Realizing all that brings in many gifts on a larger scale than you would first imagine.

When this author started this book, in the first paragraphs the focus was upon a dichotomy that has come into existence on our planet due to the great differences known in behavior of animals and plants and behavior of man. From the above work, one can see how many need in some way to start over, to regain something great that was lost, to stop infringing on the still great and perfect ways of other life forms that indeed despite our negative stance are used by man to sustain him. The dichotomy is that the behavior of man - his communications, his acts and his thoughts – are outside the normal range that our planet can really tolerate. How many murders per day exist so that man can keep feasting upon animal life and building home after home and business enterprise after business enterprise using so many resources of the Earth and its forests? Man is really living a life separate from the goodness of our world, falsely enriching himself by murder. However, we know that these riches go into hoarders' hands and are separated into dosages for groups of hoarders and their employees. Because the employees are also taken into separated thinking or into slavery as it were - into a different system of being than they would experience if left in their natural way — these more common-minded people do not fare well. Additionally, the indigenous populations that reside in areas plundered by hoarders, along with the animal and plant life there, also reside in slavery, having been cut down in their prime of life and in their continued death as it were being used so hoarders can gain wealth and high stature and to own opulent buildings and foods and belongings. These precious resources truly die and men then want more of the same to keep their thirst, unquenched, going. So we live in a world that allows or has come to accept one group lessening and doing away with another and another group. The planet somehow over time seems to accept this. But there is untold dissension because of these acts, which reflect back at man daily with round after round of negative attributes sprouting up in our land. These features we develop from our murderous acts are reflected back at us daily by far-off nonending wars. These outwardly express the hatred our planet must accept, within all of its living life, of the cruelty of man towards its animal and plant populations and also other men and women. There are many signs of this cruelty available to take in daily, seen as an outgrowth of our acts, and these signs point out the dual nature of life here - one side innately following all life's natural doings and one side unnaturally murdering the others.

What this leads to is a living planet's struggle between different whole parts of itself. And the animals are acutely aware of our malfeasance toward them. Our planet may present a different picture when we open animal conservancies and preservations, for example, and extend a loving arm, but that picture is daily destroyed by the pain of the animal slaughterhouses, a pain that is in direct contradiction to the love we say we give them. Therefore, embedded in our planet is dichotomy or confusion or love-hate behaviors, schizophrenia and other mental and then physical illnesses. In order for our planet to truly be healthy, be full with all of its gifts to own and bestow and to survive, and with its true strength, it must be free of this dichotomy of thinking. In a planet that is truly "alive," and is one living being composed of many moving parts also alive within the whole as a part of it, being alive, it can certainly become ill and even very ill. That is because people become ill, animals become ill, plants become ill, all the parts of our living planet. Then, in this author's opinion, our planet is very ill. And while the bad acts of men may have started around 6000 years ago by just a few, the unfortunate nature of their acts has flagrantly grown to cause our planet to be in a simultaneous living state of euphoria and hatred and pain and needed charity. Such conflicts mirroring back at Earthly life every day causes us to live in constant change, uncertainty, illness, fear and upheaval. One cannot endure such emotional and physical strife for long periods and unfortunately, against the nature of our living planet, many beings perish.

There are many examples evident in our daily lives giving credence to the idea that our bifurcated and dualistic world full of contradictory thoughts, words and behavior is real. Take for example the situation of the Jewish people. Jews have been persecuted on Earth for so long that the trend set of a large group of other cultures descending on another different one is not just cruel but is in many ways disturbing and contradictory. On the one hand, the Jews were the chosen people of our planet; and on another, they were routinely persecuted. What the planet knew as true was also contradicted by the feelings of groups endeavoring to persecute. No one can answer this question logically. This author asserts that this kind of disturbing contradiction in our life that seems part of emotional illness and not practical or logical thinking may be a result of dualistic thinking that has arisen since the days of Noah. Since Jews were the first organized religion, one can only infer from actions, words and thoughts running against Jews and their specific ways that large groups of our world, although adhering to ancient rituals and ways, were truly against religion. The Jewish religion believed there was only one God but the others may have believed that God existed in people. This the Jews felt was wrong. In these early days, as religion was forming and might have presented new ways of thinking, other groups of people - non-Jews - may have chosen to kill them rather than to believe in their religious tenets and in God's choice. In the case of Romans, who first started killing Jews in ancient times, they were expansionists who believed in conquering even far-off cities to take over the land there and take away power from the indigenous people of the area and make their own governing bodies and gods and goddesses supreme in these areas and to squander the local population and impoverish their hopes and dreams and ways of life, not just their physical realities. They took away everything and were especially hostile toward the Jews whose belief in one God, our Father, was sometimes detested by the polytheistic Romans. The Jews obeyed God and believed he ruled from a heavenly home. They did all they could to know Him and his desires for them and to sanctify and obey Him. The Romans on the other hand believed in many living Gods and deities who lived right among them and fought for these souls to be elevated and enriched over all men. What can be seen here as far back as Roman times is that the Romans as expansionists were hoarders and would kill for their theories to prevail while the Jews, as an agrarian group, prevailing as one community, were group thinkers. The Romans despised them and the dichotomy of our planet was there evidenced.

What happened in Rome, founded in 653 B.C., leads to one believing that indeed the dichotomy we speak of was in evidence as long ago as that time. That God had chosen the Jewish people shows His preference for group thinkers and not those who were individualists and hoarders.

However, even with God's choice in evidence, people today still choose the way of competition between them to try to gain the most individual wealth and to live by the sword of carnivorous eating. To change a society locked as it is in these behaviors seems impossible. With millions if not trillions of people partaking this way, how would we ever let go of a blood-letting world in favor of a loving one. Maybe this behavior, locked as it were, is part of an imperfection found in our world rooted in ancient early days, written and re-written somewhere somehow that cannot now be changed. Perhaps man himself did not invent these atypical choices and somehow they came about. Maybe it is up to God alone to help us either accept our loving natures along with these aberrations or to try to change these behaviors in us with the help of prayer of those who abhor the mistaken lifestyle that separates us from our truth.

Other examples of how hostile individualist thinking has torn apart group-thinking efforts throughout history involves the stories of Jesus, Martin Luther King, President Kennedy and his brother Robert, Ghandi and Nelson Mandela. Each one was stopped while in the midst of raising thinking away from individualistic tendencies toward group-thinking that involved inclusion of larger populations into the wealth and health of our planet. That so many who were so loved by large groups that were working to help large groups is indicative of the need we as a whole have against what currently prevails. But the vehemence that individualistic thinkers are capable of to keep the status quo of harmfulness upon the world also shows itself.

From the foregoing discussion, one can surmise that individual thinking is winning the day. The wealth and prosperity of our planet remains in the hands of the few while the masses oftentimes earn hardly enough to cover high rents and medical care. Many millions earn only minimum wage. The group thinkers opposing a life of inequity become doomed and are even put to death. What we know is right somehow cannot prevail, and this is a very sad and dangerous phenomenon. The mass of men not finding meaning in life due to a brutalizing hard life dummying them down to what others who own the workplaces expect of them cannot be underestimated as harrowing for our planet. True mass revolt is possible every day. This is because to go out to places designed to learn the truth of life has even become an expensive proposition often presided over by the wealthy. How often does a common man have wherewithal to learn what life can truly provide him if he chooses to seek it steadfastly. Certainly there are reading materials to guide him but for some reason the pathway home remains elusive.

What men and women can take heart in is that they do not really need money or fancy foods and homes to truly fulfill a grand destiny. It costs nothing and your diet or other circumstances do not matter. All you need to know is that finding your true path in life to great personal satisfaction and fulfillment and meaning is stored within your own body. That is true of all of us. You do not need to travel, to change your diet, to mingle with certain people, to go practice exercises that are not important to you. You simply need to know that you are from God and therefore are divine and all you need is yourself. Maybe one good practice is to spend some periods of your life alone - even if it is behind closed doors in your own room - and sit quietly or begin writing notes or simply to meditate - using as your starting point that you trust yourself to guide and teach yourself the best path to follow for coming into a life aligned with truth. Maybe in studying this, one can see a circumstance where the individual life does rule and the group can be put aside. But that does not mean your individual awakenings will lead to selfishness. What they will probably lead to is charity. And you do not have to assume that there will be a break in your life when you begin to find truth. Your life can continue as it always did, except now with greater potential for true happiness and wellbeing and health. Because as you align to your true path as desired by God your Father and the Earth your mother your life will become sublime and there will no longer be personal suffering.

In order to start a journey learning and relearning a true life for yourself you might realize that since the knowledge is already within you that you need to place importance on yourself and to like yourself. People in denial of their physical life or who suffer self-hatred need to find help to change. Once you realize how much you can truly offer yourself from yourself you need only to start understanding yourself. What are your feelings each day telling you? What realizations do you notice as you make your way each day? What things feel good to you and what feels bad? Believe that it is ok to be who you are and to value your inner thoughts, words, desires, needs. Being that you are very important to this world as a divine being, it is important that you elevate yourself in your own mind. Try to meet your needs no matter how strange or trivial they may seem. Write things down in a journal as to your reactions on a number of subjects as you make your way each day. Note if some of the things that are a part of your day bring joy or anger or dispiritedness. Learn as much as you can about yourself from all that you think and feel as you travel your own life's pathway. Write things down. Read them later. Ponder it as you lie quietly. Spend quiet time ruminating over it. These actions will lead to a long lesson later as to a blueprint of who you are and how you might become one in truth with your true life and your planet.

One of the things a greater self-awareness can give you in the detail of your life is a method to solve your problems. Sometimes we are beset with issues that have become a part of our life. They may have become a part of us from a certain age, perhaps after we finished our schooling. We live with them and in some ways skirt through certain aspects of life difficultly because of them. We may know very well our issues and have planned never to devulge them. Maybe we see a psychiatrist once a month to get around the problem. Maybe we choose to get drunk each night to avoid facing them. Maybe we even let go of some of our heartfelt hopes because we know our issues would not let us dwell well in certain happy fulfilled times and would create inner disturbance. You can make note however that having more self-awareness and practicing watching over yourself each day and writing things down about your imaginings, your responses to certain stimuli, your feelings in all situations, etc., can lead you to an awareness of yourself that even allows plans for bettering your life through learning how to implement ways to solve longstanding issues. Then these long-harassing problems can be tackled and maybe overcome.

The individual and the group aspects of being divine can be pointed out and can be shown to complement each other when used with feelings, action, words and thoughts rooted in divinity. For example, each individual is special, divine. Each individual's divinity is like a snowflake, special, unique, perfect. In and of itself, each snowflake can guide its person through all of life. Then, a second component, according to the Gaia Hypothesis, comes in. Each indginual snowflake, representing a divine intricately woven individual with his or her own capabilities, needs, hopes, dreams - an overall pathway - can also be thought of to interconnect with all other snowflakes. This allows a complementary life to unfold between all individuals, with give and take and sowing and reaping, occurring where as connected beings we give of our unique talented selves and then take from others from their unique reservoir of talented acts, thoughts and words to complement our lives similarly. Even in a world with hoarders, which are in the minority, a majority of selves, with individuality of talent and nuance, can give and take within a whole universe of others. This give and take, through Gaia, allows us to be sure that we all work rightly from our special talents to give to all others who need us what they need each day, and then to receive back in the right measure what we need and hope for from what those others' unique and individual talents can provide. This working system is divine in nature and is invisible to the naked eye. However, it most assuredly is working in all lives - expecting all people to give of themselves rightly to all those who need from him or her and to have back the same. This interconnection between people again shows how important the working group is and also adds the need for individual expression as a perfect partner when those individuals are good.

That the Gaia Hypothesis comes about from the divinity of all life through an interconnected way between all life, including plant and animal life, shows that not only is our Earth method reliant on living beings but that the living being the biosphere and all of its special unique parts are also divine - as a whole. Being alive in a way is in and of itself such a gift it is divine. And the proof that our planet is alive is that within every space of existence as far as the eye can see there is life - fireflies, birds, leafy plants, insects, bears and tigers and elephants, people, children, adults, teenagers, trees and grass to name only a very few. That some misguided hoarding individuals would want to kill whole classes of life, for example, the whole Jewish race and so many million cows, every day, is a complete reversal of thinking in regard to who we truly are. And it is important to realize that in a world of unique individual life, with each and every life as intricately different from another as a snowflake differs from another snowflake, that to lose even one part of the magnificent whole is heartbreaking. Something unique that cannot be replaced might be gone from us. If even one person or plant or animal is lost the picture of life is no longer complete and we are left empty with a small hole unfillable.

Sometimes you look at your life and you think, I wish had done something differently. Or, I should have done better in school, I should have held on to that friend, why did I not take that job opportunity. These types of thoughts show a lack of satisfaction with yourself and your life. They also show an embarrassment or dissatisfaction with your circumstances. However, the things you chose instead during the times you did not choose the things you regret not having chosen were a part of you. And being a divine being you can say to yourself, I think I made the right choice at the time. And, maybe a choice I will make tomorrow will be what I now hope for. When you begin to understand your divine nature, the kinds of nagging thoughts that brought you self disparagement will no longer be so prevalent because it is ok to believe in who you are and not who you must attain to be. It's ok to even believe in your outwardly seeming most grotesque thoughts and know that they are accepted. Instead of self denial, believe in self acceptance. Then build something from a firm foundation every day. Somehow we are taught that to be enough is to have a certain amount of money, a perfect marriage, a grand home and car. But these media campaigns mostly come from individual thinkers and not group thinkers. Group thinkers can know that even though they chose to serve in the military and serve and protect and even did a good job but perhaps came home broken, they still worked from within divinity. They can know coming home broken and aged is their reward for a job well done and they can then wait for the community at home to welcome them and heal them. Maybe also your mother was a beautiful soul but crippled with self-doubt and alcoholism. Perhaps you chose to love her unconditionally instead of dragging her to doctors. You can rest on your choices instead of condemning yourself to please others. Part of being divine is trusting yourself and loving yourself. Your actions do not have to look good in the newspaper or on television but need to please you and those you care for. In fact, leading a pleasing life for yourself and your immediate neighbors or family is of utmost importance. Such a set of choices are well within divinity. In fact, any such nice behavior that simply expresses the life and energy God gives you sweetly and not with hostility is divine behavior. Believe in creating a beautiful nesting environment at home. Believe in nurturing your daily needs. Believe in kindness and friendliness to your neighbors. Even broken with self doubt smile in the mirror each morning and smile at your friend who always was there in the house next door. Say hello always. Believe you are worthy of greatness and not someone the world says is ugly. Never believe that you acted wrongly. Just act as greatly as you can right now. All this advice is pointed toward finding your true nature and your innately honest nature and abiding by it. And this author feels that all men's true and natural behavior is from good, not evil. What people might need to remember is that their good is reconnecting with our mother, the Earth, and saying she must be helping me today and then do everything you can to see your group and not just yourself. Another point to make is that when your divine self makes choices and behaves in certain ways that later come to you as ugly things you were partaking of, know that at the time you might have been suffering illness and that your body, mind and soul may not have been completely well. Pray to find ways to heal so that your own behavior will not disappoint you again. Healing can be found in simply finding reading material that stands out to you as important. When you at times look back and see behaviors you indulged in that you know were wrong, just say that you must accept them because they expressed your true self at the time. Who you were then, even mistakenly, was just you. That doesn't mean people should stop loving you or being your friend. Even in your ugliest moments you can say I was just being me. And you do not need to go further than that. Another thought that might cross your mind is that in your current state you could not possibly be divine yet and that divinity is a thing you must attain or that men do not seem divine right now because of the state of their acts, words and thoughts. However, that could not be more wrong. You do not ever have to attain to be divine because you are. And divinity does not look different than what is being currently seen and expressed; divine is who everyone is right now in their current state, expressing all of their acts, words and thoughts. We may be living in a veiled time where our true specialness is hidden to us or is veiled; however, everything we do, think or say expresses our divine nature.

One might ordinarily think we are an ugly world. There is war, drug addiction, alcoholism, prejudice, strife. Why do we as men and women express such barbarism? A lot of the answer goes back to being turned away since the times of the Great Flood from our true nature, maybe turned to the side of it, not wanting to accept it, in a sense turning away from God. But even the actions and thoughts and words associated with all of that expresses ourselves, still divine. Somehow there is a barrier that has grown between our divine selves and our planet and we are left standing alone. How do we reconfigure our way home? You may think divinity should look differently than all of that and you must attain it, and divinity is just different from what is. But that could not be more wrong. Everything that is, everything you do, say and think expresses you and you, as divine, express divine individuality and your divine interconnectedness with your group. If there is a barrier grown that too came from a divine mind. You do not need to find the path to divinity, you do not need to find anything. Divinity lies within you and you must only find or better know yourself. In fact, going on a journey to find yourself only adds a bunch of things to you, maybe things that take you out of yourself and into new adventures. The true way is to let many things outside yourself fall away and let you as an individual be the adventure, not so many things you might enjoy to think of instead of that. Pairing down your life to let who you are stand out more clearly shows better judgment.

The problem with asserting your divine self is that our planet is stuck in a systematic state of truth and lie. The truth that all animals and plants are pure and that they operate on all measures entwined with the planet and its needs and rewards is a foundation that we rely on. The truth of their being is that they are systematically a part of all elemental cycles of Earth. On the other hand, man - while also having a set of behaviors, language and thoughts that are deeply rooted now in our world and operating throughout our ebbing and flowing as systematic - lives outside the true nature of our world and robs from it. Sometimes it is hard to point out the culprit because the activities of man became systematic a long time ago. The planet's life is skeptical of man's pathway and knows he is a destructive force forming a destructive cycling. How then to assert your divinity. The answer is that you must align your thoughts, deeds and words with Gaia and never go back. You must work every day to find and fine tune your true divine nature. Without starting this process and sticking with it to show God and our Earth Mother our true intentions, we will surely die. The fact is our belligerent false embedded systematic behaviors bring on death in our world to men. To animals and plants we do not know but, in this author's opinion, they are eternal. Men, on the other hand, operating in this way, are not. but a divine being, this author believes, could be, if hls or her acts, thoughts and words would only align to Earth law.

After man had changed and began sacrificing animals and turned away from his innate connectivity with the true Earth system, his being over the ages from difficult acts and words and thoughts changed. The divine in him may have become covered over. Somehow his life turned to violence instead of peace. In this author's opinion, man was still divine but began not to know it so much. He may have even been closed to his true nature rather than be open, and this decision may have come from a higher power. If God visited man and showered love on him for his divine nature man may have been mystified as to what the loving gifts were for. He may have asked for a gift or have prayed for a joyful meal at the end of the day however. But the nature of his divinity was not known to him. His true calling may have become hidden as if veiled. Many changes throughout the ages occurred, and it was probably the jobs of the scribes of the time to make heads or tails out of what men would do each day. Something had been lost and elders may have become more important to guide a changed population.

Once man was disconnected from his innate sense, his lack of knowing what to do, think and say caused him to rely on others to guide him, this author believes, as stated above. His planet may not have had as much for him as he made new choices. A great example of new forms of guidance coming about for man is the Bible, which promises man many things for the time when he is ready and one assumes that means ready to think universally again and to reconnect to the old ways. The Bible is a precious book given to all men, professed to be written by God, to help man through his manifold troubled times.

This one artifact surpassed all others in giving man a guide as to what God needed him to do, think and say during the troubling years after the catastrophes. The book showed that religion and education were extremely necessary for men of those times so that their ways could be retrained back to feeling love again, allowing their evolution to occur rightly with the pathway of the planet. The book told men that although they may be blinded, that did not mean that they were not good. However, when God took the hand of man to calm and heal him, he also knew that men were blinded to their true divinity. That lack of knowledge of their true self happened and God became everything to men. At this present time in history, however, men can begin to realize themselves and to study their self. This will lead to the truths of our planet and its place for men to be revealed, which will bring back the stature of men and the chance to find life eternal.

It seems that man may finally be tired of war and persecution and weapons of mass destruction. lt seems that man may be tired of journeying far from his family to enrich himself somehow somewhere far away. Man need not travel so much. There is a great wealth in the comfort of a home that one might inhabit not for a few short years but for lifetimes. Within this kind of environment, man truly can come to study and learn and educate himself to live a more gifted and truthful life. And this possible awakening would be coming none too soon. That is because one-third of the Earth now is classified as desert land, including cold and hot deserts, cities covered over with asphalt and the polar regions. These areas are labeled this way because within their confines vegetation cannot grow; they are inhospitable areas where animal life is not prevalent. These have come about from man's unmerciful killing of forests, other vegetation and animals. Instead of desert, this one-third of our planet's land could be flourishing with immeasurable wealth. This is a goal that should be set in place, to start to rebuild and reclaim our amazing planet. One should note that in the negative onslaught that the mass merchants pursue to tear down precious forests for the making of plastic products and toaster ovens and the like, they leave behind a very sad emblem in the places once flourishing but now gone. All of the animal and insect life that lived and flourished in these areas were brought to a sudden cataclysmic reality that broke up their habitats and daily work and scattered their families far afield. The pain they suffered and may still suffer is hard to quantify. What then is left is a one-part hostile population with no knowledge of what they have done to a now frightened and belittled other group. This is again another example of the polarity of ways between man and the natural world, leaving part of the Earth's living being in a state of catatonic catastrophe with deep wounds in their psyches. That becomes a part of us, of every living part of the planet to share. To build back a desecrated land area may be for man to do after such a series of terrifying encounters with the once-wondrous natural world. In those areas what now remains may be calamitous sadness and fear.

To have populations of the earth angry and frightened of other populations is probably a phenomenon not calculated for in the early days of man. For such a phenomenon to arise was not planned, in this author's opinion. How to cope with a callous and brutal murderous approach to natural life by man? It is terrifying to gentler souls who would do anything to be free of this. The world population that would be opposed to such doings needs to join together in some form of forceful awakening against these atrocities. It may be the only way to survive.

Finally, since we know that the Earth is alive, we can note that some things common to man - for example, having emotions - could also be common to other life and the life of our planet. Our Earthly soul may feel just as the desecrated animal and plant populations feel. Our holistic planet may feel dejection, sadness, uncertainty, fear, a lack of hope - all reflected from the millions of life forms now squandered. This puts a pall on all of us and gives us an emotional toll to carry. Just how many men and women suffer from depression would be a good question to ponder.

When it comes time to give of oneself to change this bad course we are on, our own blackened emotions may cause us to feel unable to help. The mirroring back to each of us of our wrongful deeds, words or thoughts is very real. The life we create for ourselves and others - including any death toll or desecration - must be shouldered by those involved. For the gaining of material wealth, the burden earned equally may be more than one bargained for and may shut down a possibly productive and happy life.

This idea of part of the Earth operating from malicious disregard and the other from fear says a lot about the wealth of our planet. A truly prosperous planet hums along every moment with sowing activities and then reaping of reward. The sowing helps all of the world and the reaping happens as one completes a cycle of sowing. And in this correctly functioning world so many gifts bringing so much happiness are possible. This is the crux of the Gaia hypothesis. But what good can all sowing each day be when sowed into our lives and livelihoods is either maliciousness and greed and on the other side of the coin a feeling of lack and pain. The two do not coalesce well. The side feeling pain and fear will alert in their daily working activities to the other side the cruelty they endure and the other side will degrade the suffering further, possibly making the hoarding selfish types dig their heels in. From the work of both of these types not much good can occur. The work is imbued with fractured emotions and will not lead to a divine perfection that we are all certainly capable of. This causes a bigger problem on our planet. And that is because the animals' habitat tending processes within their sowing activities are weakened. The buildup of pollution and weather calamities are results that show this current state of our affairs and how they affect our world discordantly. Secondly, within the Gaia hypothesis is the idea that all are connected and thus reap and sow with each other and for each other because we know and care for each other as families, friends and neighbors. All life is included. This need for connectivity to assure all are cared for on Earth might be a harder task today, what with so much hostility and fear present between opposing groups. The groups may prefer to remain severed from each other and this preference can lead to disaster. Then the parts of the Earth suffering will continue to degrade and suffer further while the hoarding aggressors will probably build monuments to their wealth in more and more urban-style environments. That the wild aspect of the Earth is being shunted by those who build forever more cities and towns will eventually play out with all things crumbling. The reason for that is each city and town truly depends on wilderness to survive, just as much as many broken parts of the Earth depend on man to come through for them. For example, the four seasons and the climate which we all know we need as temperate comes from wilder parts of our terrain. What will happen with a lessened health in those. Animals truly have a role in the natural world habitat and the climate and season and weather arise from their work in the wilder areas. These directly impact our lives even far afield. We cannot neglect the demand that an unhealthy world puts upon us to act. For example, when Al Gore envisioned "Climate Reality" he couldn't have come along at a better time. The changes our planet has undergone from his work and his groups' efforts cannot be ignored. The pleasure he has brought man, vegetation and animal cannot be measured it is so great and the education he has fostered as to the connection between all parts of the Earth and their dependence upon each other to survive well has also been clearly shown.

That rocks and trees and an ocean, lake or stream have emotions is hard to fathom. However, habitats such as these are brimming with life. They become alive through the breathing within them of their inhabitants. They are known - habitats - to become oxygenated by teeming animal life within. If the wildlife sees its habitats plundered and family members lost they most certainly feel strong emotions about such a series of events. The soil they live within expresses feelings as do trees for animals that dwell in such. People cannot grasp the harsh reality they have inflicted upon the animal kingdom which does so much to keep our Earth green, growing, temperate and hygienic. Why would we be so ruthless to their families and dwellings. We must acknowledge what our business enterprises are doing to these creatures and what our purchased products amount to in terms of lost life and home. And when trees and other vegetation are taken and precious freshwater supplies are contaminated the animal populations of the area are left without food and water, suddenly thrown fearful and adrift after possibly centuries of living within those now torn up environs. The karma that comes back to us simply reflects what we have done first. Sometimes you see an animal pick out one man in a group to negatively harass. You might wonder why. But an animal is a gifted higher being and he may know something of that chosen soul's doings that impacted him. One might have to admit to a war being in place everyday on Earth between animal and man as chickens, cows and pigs are slaughtered on a routine basis.

Our planetary truths are based on holism, meaning all Earth's living forms, for example, make up a whole. And the whole in and of itself - not just the life forms within it - is important as a living being - albeitly multifaceted. This whole being - all of us together, including all animal and sea life, humans and vegetation - being alive within a living sphere of our planet, the biosphere, represent a living whole that interacts in ways that affect all others, giving and taking and helping to sustain life as a whole. Being alive inside this whole being, all of us, there is hardship to see who acts along the philosophy of obeying the needs of a planetary whole and those that operate from a different viewpoint. However, this is probably important to our creator and probably shows all of our systematic unstable behaviors. In some ways our whole may be forever changing even while regulatory cycling runs through it. These changes give us hope that Earth can accept change and if and when man decides to change the planet might find a total healing possible. Feelings also from one part of the whole can be experienced far afield In another part where our sensitivity - which still does prevail - feels pain and upset of others. From this idea one can surmise that we know each other well. Sometimes a whole group will share emotions together as is the case when a beloved public figure dies. On the occasions that the world suffered the loss of some of its very public people, government leaders or movie stars, for example, the sharing of emotion in response is palpable. It is in times like these that we feel not just our pain but the pain of our neighbors; this highlights our true collective nature. In addition, when a cultural phenomenon occurs, such as the counter-cultural movement of the 1950s, many joined others together to adopt similar ideals in their lives. Together this greatly-numbered group shared many ideas and emotions all together. This group tended to lead happy lives. They shared so much in thought, words and deeds. Other cultural groups would include soldiers, for example, all trained in the same way for the military and therefore very alike each other. These groups share thoughts and emotions and feel what others feel among them. And they are known to stand well together to support each other and feel the pain of one another in a truly synchronously harmonized whole. This - as stated in the Gaia Hypothesis - shows how in these few prevalent group models, the participants shared feelings and thoughts and formed a holistic being consisting of all of its members, which became then a larger whole. They became successfully run group-thinking ideals because the actors within each group came from a loving place for other members of their group. Love is all a group needs to succeed as being alive with good sowing and reaping along the lines of Gaia's thinking. These two groups, those of the 1960s counter-culture and those of the military, spoken of above, formed positive wells of human behavior against the hoarding individualists. And these groups flourish because they have many positive beliefs that tie them with others of similar thinking. In no part of a group culture can a negative system flourish - that takes away sustenance from another to bring inordinately more sustenance to someone who already might have a lot - without dire consequences. But somehow we have shown that this happens on the larger scale. As a whole therefore we are still ridden with inconsistencies, contradictions, dualities, truth and lies. It is easy to see how many might become mentally ill due to this dualism so strongly a part of our being within the living Earth. We therefore express in our own lives many inconsistencies, contradictions and dualistic attitudes. This inconsistent reality means our planet is reflecting a powerful negative truth that becomes a part of us, and our wellbeing is affected. We want to be good people, but along the way in life, most begin to go wrong. We may be choosing this impact or it may be that that reality is thrust upon us. From this illness many seek help. Many see doctors, chiropractors, therapists, masseuses, hypnotherapists, nutritionists, etc. And what they are really doing is trying to find out why they are unhappy and unfulfilled and unhealthy. They want to lead better lives. However, the cause of the upset is unknown to them. What people must realize is that these steps taken to better one's life are good steps to take that might lead to a later realization of the true origins of individual life problems. Later, among those healing, there might even be exertion to heal others and possibly even our planet. Usually a healed soul will become one with gratitude and a charitable soul and then some changes might occur. Another way that one may measure the level of togetherness our planet can offer is to examine a population after a national calamity occurs. Usually, when a natural catastrophe occurs, such as a flood, people join others and seem to instinctively know who rise to become leaders to help the group and who are fallen who need help. Often, every life is saved. This is evidence of how strongly our emotions can be tied to one another and experienced.

There is one major problem that seems almost impossible to change, however, and this represents a facet of our lives that causes much illness in us that we are not free to relinquish: the phenomenon is that we as a population are more cow than human. We eat so much from the cow's life - the bodies of cows and their outputs like milk and cheese that are there for the cows' young, the calves. We crave things also that might not be craved if we only were acting from a proper human diet. There are so many dead cows in humans that the problem means rethinking things that have gone down a longstanding path. Our diet if changed to what would be truly meant for man might be the best remedy toward healing our world over anything. This change would stop the slaughter of animals and that is the crux of our major problem.

Throughout this book I've touched on many ideas - the heart of which relate to the truthful way we are meant to follow on our planet. A truthful path for life on Earth, a living planet, could never involve murder. One may wonder, however, how some might know what the true meaning of their lives entails. But we can easily deduce anything in life, its truths and ways versus falsehoods and wrong turns, by turning to our own selves for knowledge. How do we feel when we see another person or an animal get hurt? When we are shown that much of the tropical rain forests are in jeopardy how do we react? Our feelings about the myriad subjects that run through our lives every day are clear signs of the meaning the things we encounter every day have for us. And sometimes there is great contradiction. For example, we may enjoy the things we buy from the superstore but then at the same time regret that part of the Earth may have been hurt in the manufacturing of these. We do enjoy cooking beef and chicken and pork but at the same time profess a love of the animal. This on a grand scale influencing the thinking and being of a whole population has tremendous impact, and from these feelings a dualism grows in our population and, through that strength of dual feelings, this also is felt within each individual, and contradictory pathways of being for each and every one of us are created. Everything we need to know about our true path, our true way - the meaning of our life - can be known from what we feel and do and think and communicate, and just what we do from the age when we begin to care for ourselves away from our parents might be broken into pieces. Finding your own inner truth to live by is not so difficult if one is honest with oneself about these issues and understands the true consequences of our ways of life. The contradiction that we enjoy things that hurt others - for example, the animals that died so we could have our lunch and dinner or the loss of forest so that we can have our perfectly decorated and equipped kitchens - leads to unhappiness and unhealthiness in us. And there is a veil in many people who do not see the connection between what they do every day and another life far off suffering for it. Then the dangerous phenomenon of populations marked with feelings of fear, sadness, anger, apathy and a general unhealthy mental state occurs because in the larger sense those souls hurt by our doings are feeling that way and we feel it too because the immense number of hurt souls creates a large emotional toll felt by a whole world.

And there is confusion in the natural world in as much of it as there is in ours, the world of man. This is because we truly love nature, scenic travels, animal life, our pets at home. Then suddenly somewhere else the cows are innumerably murdered. People may see no clear reason for their own share of the pain nor any way to alleviate it. But if they truly knew their own part of the whole they could begin to understand that they must change. This is because the connection

between our daily choices and the suffering elsewhere because of these is in most cases not truly understood, and that is why disease and mental illness are not clearly understood. This causes a cycle to continue in us - to seek help in a myriad of ways to alleviate and heal our suffering and estrangement without ever truly finding real healing- on a nonending basis. The best thing to do to alleviate pain in life is to be aware of the habits of your life that indeed hurt others. When you hurt another person or animal or even a plant, their living soul will know about it. If you are continuously watchful for such activities you might change forms of behavior that are detrimental. Then the path to happiness and better mental health is possible.

When one considers the idea that within the whole Earth living being two large almost all-inclusive groups are at war, as humans continue to slaughter animals and animals are forced to accept this, one might realize that a hatred exists from this phenomenon, leading to bursts of anger from within our planet. These bursts are so full of hostility that it engulfs our entire world. Then when perhaps we think we are going to war to save Israel, for example, in reality we may be going to war to save ourselves against angry indigenous populations who for the continued slaughter that benefits our tables, we must come out to see the ramifications. This is our own karma coming back to us. Other forms of hatred come out as well, such as youths yearning for violence in their lives when their parents only wish better for them. Gang violence, for example, is an outgrowth of a generally felt anger existing on our planet - this general anger latent in us and our youth comes, this author believes, from man's need to keep animal slaughter and the criminal behavior toward natural ecosystems going.

The only way this author sees as the path to ending violence and subsequent illness in our lives is to become a population more self aware of its actions, thoughts, feelings and communications and always the true consequences of such. If one truly understood the consequences for all of their choices, one would see how their specific troubles arose. It is important for people to be aware of all of their daily doings and how these might impact another soul whether near or far. The true path to enjoying a great healthy life is self awareness leading to self enlightenment. The ability to attain these are built within your own bodies; you need not travel far to attain. And then once you begin learning of yourself and having realizations regarding your daily actions, you can begin to 1) enter a life or a group of lives without harming others, and 2) experience true change in your daily actions, feelings, thoughts and communications that heal your life. Because you cannot change your course if you think it is a good one, albeit with illness, as easily as you can change it when you are truly aware of all of the specific and general ramifications that each action, thought and communication emanating from you has, it is better to live troubled and even tormented for what you have done wrong rather than to live sublimely. That is the path of healing. And when true change comes in, we can say we finally have the knowledge to be on a more truthfully divine life course with true happiness and health as a beneficial result.

Finally, one might say that for a successful living system such as our planet to truly evolve well that that system must operate with love. Indeed, sowing and reaping is meant for a sharing population and much sharing and working for others among large diverse groups. This kind of sharing, that is there to aid our very survival, comes from love. The word "evolve" truly contains the word love within it. Can you say you really love animals if you are a part of the separation of their families and the killing of their lives for our sustenances? You really cannot say that any Ionger. In order to restore love, one must watch their daily doing, thinking and communicating in order to find where they stand as far as living a loving life. Their goal must be to become truly loving of our world and respectful of all beings within it. Then humans might heal their fractured souls. The implication of living outside the planetary law and making life choices alone without guidance from the planet and a whole population of others - your family on Earth - that might have helped you to make better healthier choices seems frightening. Since man in many ways chose not to be guided by the natural planet which contains also plant and animal thinking who then would guide men, he traveled away from truth and knowledge. Men seek to guide themselves with falsehoods. Where then since man is turned this way does men's learning come from you might ask, and that answer might be the school room. But in many cases, man might have to admit that much of his learning also comes from the churches, synagogues and mosques. These are places that offer guidance; however, religion states that it's espoused truths and knowledge come from God. (The Bible comes to mind, which is said to have been written by God.) Therefore, man is adding to his learning through the religious teachings of God. This may be the case but what is neglected to be mentioned is that man, despite this, chooses to remain false, crippled with actions that go against common sense and knowledge of our living planet given in the school subjects and also in church. Because both schools and churches were made by man, the learned content is tailored by man and not expressing the true nature of our separated planet.

One might add in regard to the notion of our lives and our planet exhibiting dualism that a once richly sublime working of a biosphere of life sowing and reaping and helping each other may now - due to our contemptuous feelings toward animal and plant life and due to a skepticism that may have arisen among animal life toward humans - not hold the same potential or promise for perfection. There may be in place of much of our planet's perfection a disorder and chaos where what might have been in place was a better working system. However, this author strenuously disagrees that mind and body of man and animal are dualistic naturally. The state of perfection exists and will always exist and, during which time when this perfection can somehow show itself, one will see that all beings of our planet want to truly heal and match up well with each other. Finally, one might say that while we act in ways that seem enduringly wrong, within us all still exists our perfection. Even in a world crippled with dualism we must admit that our planet is rooted in holism. Another aspect of man containing dualities might arise from the sharing together with others of oxygen which we spoke of earlier in this book. Part of each of our being may have transferred into many others' beings through the sharing that occurs on a living planet. This form of dualism is rooted in our very nature and is good and adds hope that as a whole unified force man can change.

In the end one must agree that there is a clear difference between good and evil - and the dualism of our planet reflects that difference - and that knowing the difference comes from the simplest form of analyzing that is possible. There is simply no excuse for committing evil acts when a person would in most cases know well what they are doing. That creates a second evil attached to the original action. When choosing evil the flow of Gaia into your life would have to lessen and your health would not be as good. And the sad thing is that evil can spread like a fire, hard to quell, when it is rooted in, say, a mother or father of children who always would try in their early years to emulate the behavior of their parents and therefore may have been thrust into evil with many reinforcing emotions from the parents' actions, thoughts and words to hammer nails into a coffin over almost a lifetime. It is up to man to try and recover these lost families, because what is the alternative?

The curing of our ills may seem an impossible task but it takes only a few dedicated souls to make a dent in the armor of indifference. When friends of changed individuals see changes in a positively changing other, they too may start making amendments in their lifestyle toward positive change. This author truly hopes that this book becomes a guiding light in that long pathway home.

In the end I can only say thank you for reading my book and I and will pray for you